A Brief History of Jazz Rock

A Brief History of Jazz Rock

Mike Baron

WordFire Press
Colorado Springs, Colorado

A BRIEF HISTORY OF JAZZ ROCK
Copyright © Mike Barron, 2014

All rights reserved. No part of this book may be reproduced or transmitted in any form or by any electronic or mechanical means, including photocopying, recording or by any information storage and retrieval system, without the express written permission of the copyright holder, except where permitted by law. This novel is a work of fiction. Names, characters, places and incidents are either the product of the author's imagination, or, if real, used fictitiously.

ISBN: 978-1-61475-148-9

Book Design by RuneWright, LLC
www.RuneWright.com

Published by
WordFire Press, an imprint of
WordFire, Inc.
PO Box 1840
Monument, CO 80132

Kevin J. Anderson & Rebecca Moesta Publishers

WordFire Press Trade Paperback Edition 2014
Printed in the USA
www.wordfire.com

INTRODUCTION

I like to read about music. I scour *Rolling Stone*, *Guitar Player*, *Under the Radar*, *Spin* and anything else within reach and go immediately to the record reviews. I'm looking for new sounds, and I want to know what they sound like before I listen. This is not a contradiction but the basis of commercial art. People want what they know in a slightly different form. Revenge movies: *Death Wish*, *Nevada Smith*, *Harry Brown*. Situation comedies: *Father Knows Best*, *The Brady Bunch*, *Married... with Children*, *Modern Family*. Food: Swiss cheeseburger, American cheeseburger, mushroom cheeseburger.

I follow jazz and power pop. If the writer is any good, I can tell in an instant how the band sounds. Artists have reviled critics since the first caveman drew a wooly mammoth on the wall. Miles Davis called them scum. But without critics (or the softer term reviewers), a lot of bands would never attract an audience. We live in an age where things go viral at any second. The market is swift and brutal.

Many reviewers play the simile game. Sounds like the Beatles. The Zep. U2. *Alternative Press* and *CMJ* provide a "Sounds Like" box at the end of each review. Artists naturally resent any attempt to label them or compare them. Nevertheless, music writers and musicians are joined in a symbiotic relationship. It's always easier to put something down than to praise it for two reasons:

knocking something is fun and all the praise language has been used up. Negative reviews appeal to our baser instincts. Positive reviews are harder.

Writing, too, is an art and any writer worth his laptop strives to use fresh language to describe that which is fresh.

There's a condition called synesthesia in which a person receives sensory input and the mind switches it into another sense. Someone listening to the Beatles, for example, might experience the music as a kaleidoscope of color. Someone staring at red walls may smell bacon. Writers are synesthesiacs by nature. We are always trying to describe experiences with words, no matter how ill suited words are to the task. We are alchemists in reverse, rendering priceless ephemera into prosaic words.

My goal is to introduce the reader to the forgotten world of jazz rock and give an idea how the music sounds. That is why I describe so many songs in detail.

I have tried to tell this story chronologically. Sorta. Bands appear to die then come roaring back in unexpected configurations. Bands become institutions and periodically tour with one or two of the original members as bonafides. Some of the greatest jazz rock bands are semi-active today without any original members. Blood, Sweat and Tears comes to mind. On the other hand, Tower of Power still tours with original members 40 years after its inception.

Most of jazz rock happened from '68 to '72. By then it was over except for the legacy bands.

The Big Bang—the sixties—released a pent-up yearning for freedom and optimism that has sadly fallen from favor in today's balkanized music world. Band after band touches on social responsibility, none more than Chicago with songs like "Someday," "It Better End Soon," and "Dialogue." The Sons of Champlin: "Hey Children." Jam Factory: "It's Your World." The Rascals: "People Got to be Free," "A Ray of Hope" (written for Robert F. Kennedy), and "Right On." Electric Flag: "Killing Floor" (Howlin' Wolf).

Many of those bands would not and do not recognize the modern music world with its downloads, file sharing and bands offering their wares free over the web. The corporate music world is dying. CD sales have been diminishing every year since 2003. Shows like *American Idol* value technique over content and steer their contestants to middle of the road FM fare.

Every program establishes a constituency. Years ago in Florida a cable television channel went temporarily off the air. The company broadcast videos of goldfish in an aquarium for sixty days while they reorganized. When they went back on the air, viewers phoned to complain that they missed the fish and wanted them back.

The number of classic bands who have inspired youngsters continues to grow. Beatles imitators are legion. The Beach Boys have a growing and powerful following spearheaded by Explorers Club. Grateful Dead jam-type bands cover the hills. The Quarter After worship the Byrds. But one group is conspicuously missing. Where are the new jazz rock bands?

Fortunately, the Sons of Champlin, Malo and Tower of Power are still with us. Chicago and BS&T periodically reform and go on tour. The economics of keeping a big band on the road are daunting and if income is down, people are less inclined to pay forty-five bucks a ticket and drive sixty miles. I hope that young jazz rockers will read the book, listen to the music and heed the call.

Many people helped with this book including Mark Williams the airline pilot, and Bruce Brodeen the impresario. Andy Kuhn contributed the cover graphic and Mike Kilroy did the design.

As usual, this book would not exist with the help and support of my wonderful wife Ann.

CHAPTER 1
FROM OUT OF THE BLUES

Jazz rock began, like so many cultural and political movements, in the late sixties. The musical explosion that happened in the wake of the Beatles was the Big Bang, hurling music in a million different directions. Artists turned giddy with freedom of expression and a thousand bands bloomed.

Some followed the Beatles. Some stuck to the blues. Some practiced that good ol' Brill Building magic, an esthetic that informs hundreds of bands today. It was only natural that rock artists begin to explore the possibilities of jazz. After all, Miles Davis was exploring the possibilities of rock with his groundbreaking *Bitches Brew* and subsequent albums. Mingus drummer Danny Richmond played in Mark-Almond, and for Elton John. Elvin Jones drummed for a rock band called The Insect Trust along with sax player Robert Palmer who later became a noted rock critic.

Jazz rock is The Butterfield Blues Band, John Mayall's Bluesbreakers, Seatrain, Blood, Sweat & Tears, Chicago, Dreams, If, Colosseum, The Electric Flag, the Flock, Jam Factory, Silhouette, and Metamorphosis (a seventies band not related to the current band of the same name), among others.

A Brief History of Jazz Rock

It began in 1965 with The Sons of Champlin. (The Sons were not initially jazz rock, but let us chart their progress over the years.) The Sons had a four-man horn section prompting one observer to call them "acid jazz." The seminal year of '67 saw the formation of Blood, Sweat and Tears, the Chicago Transit Authority (later Chicago). It was the year Butterfield added horns and Mike Bloomfield quit Butter to form The Electric Flag.

R&B outfits have always featured dirty sax and swayful back-up hewing to R&B juice dive conventions. Whether you call it jazz rock, jazz, rock, or rhythm and blues, it all began, as so much American music did, with the blues.

If you don't know about the blues, you are probably not reading this book. For the rest of us, the blues are like pornography. We may not be able to define it, but we know it when we hear it. Of course the blues are easy to define: twelve bars, three chords, first, fourth, and fifth. You can dissect the blues, but like humor or a frog, it dies in the process.

The blues is more of a feeling. Ain't nothin' but a good man feelin' bad. Technique is a given. It's soul that counts. Technique was a basic requirement to enter the gladiatorial cauldron of blues in the twentieth century, more so for jazz. Any player who hadn't mastered his instrument or sang off-key got crashed right off the stage. The drummer would throw a cymbal on the floor and the shamed poetaster would slink off to (a) never show his face in a juke joint again, or (b) vow to master his instrument no matter what it took—including a deal with the devil. Both Robert Johnson and Charlie Parker were said to have cut that deal. Maybe Hendrix. (Walter Hill's movie *Crossroads* deals with this premise.)

Blues has always been big on the Chitlin Circuit, but it wasn't until the sixties that it began to make inroads with the white listening audience. Whites had been listening to gentrified blues for years. Elvis singing Big Mama Thornton's "Hound Dog." Pat Boone singing Fats Domino's "Ain't That a Shame." Janis Joplin singing Erma Franklin's "Piece of My Heart." Of course, all three of those songs were written by white boys, but you get the point.

Blues raised its profile in the sixties when British rock sensations the Rolling Stones drew attention to their influences and spoke reverently of their debt to the blues in interviews. While America was going gaga for the Beatles, Britain was going gaga for the blues. Performers like Long John Baldry and Blues Incorporated paved the way for bands such as the Rolling Stones, Led Zeppelin and Fleetwood Mac.

Such was John Mayall's passion for the blues he named his band the Blues Breakers. *The Blues Breakers Featuring Eric Clapton* captures the moment.

In the United States, Mayall had a counterpart in Paul Butterfield, son of a Hyde Park attorney, who gravitated to Chicago's South Side where he sat at the feet of Muddy Waters, Little Walter, and Otis Spann.

Both Mayall and Butterfield fulfilled the dictum, "ontogeny recapitulates phylogeny." Each band recreated the history of the emergence of jazz from blues in miniature. Butter got there first but Mayall was quick to follow.

Jazz rock took flight in the latter sixties as blues bands, most notably the Paul Butterfield Blues Band and the Blues Project went through painful but creative transformation. As Butterfield begat The Electric Flag and Full Moon, so the Blues Project begat Blood, Sweat, and Tears and Seatrain.

From out of left field came the Sons of Champlin, a loosey-goosey eleven-man band with four horns that blazed fresh trails in jazz rock due to their ignorance of the blues. Ironically, Bill Champlin would go on to fully embrace rhythm & blues and its intellectual cousin jazz. The Sons of Champlin are active today, but in different form from the original. Tower of Power, born across the bay in Oakland, came at rock from the opposite direction—straight from jump blues. Malo, also from the Bay Area, started out as the Malibus, an R&B cover band but by the time they found their footing had embraced Afro-Cuban jazz.

From center field came Chicago's The Flock, and Chicago themselves. Not every band with horns qualifies as jazz/rock. The Ides of March used horns most notably on "Vehicle," but the rote charts and lack of improv disqualify this as hybrid.

Do horns make a rock band jazzy? No, but the bulk of these bands incorporate horns. Jazz bands slumming don't count. Fusion groups such as Chick Corea's Return to Forever or Larry Coryell's The Eleventh House came at rock from jazz, mostly incorporating a hard rock rhythm section with an electric bass. If they don't feature vocals, they're not jazz rock. It's the vocals that make the jazz rock *rock*. Jazz rock has strong pop elements.

Whereas jazz sometimes seems too hip for its own good, jazz rock casts a wider net. The jazz rock bands wanted hits. Some got them. One could argue that jazz rock wasn't up to the standards of jazz—compare Chicago trombonist James Pankow with Curtis Fuller, for example. But Pankow's achievement in integrating the trombone into a rock band may have greater impact. He certainly casts a wider net than Fuller.

There's a reason it's called pop. Jazz rock as pop tries to reach as wide an audience as possible. Jazz seems insular by comparison.

Two key jazz ingredients are technical prowess and improvisational ability. It's fair to ask how well these guys play their axes and whether or not they can jam.

It is instructive to observe two different bands from different lands that followed remarkably similar paths: the Butterfield Blues Band and John Mayall's Blues Breakers. Both leaders were passionate about the blues and determined to bring the music to a wider audience.

CHAPTER 2
THE BUTTEREVOLUTION

Paul Butterfield grew up in Chicago and began hanging with Muddy Waters, Otis Spann, and Little Walter, from whom he learned the harmonica, at age eighteen. Butterfield met Elvin Bishop in 1961 when the eighteen-year-old Tulsa native arrived for his freshman year at the University of Chicago. Elvin Bishop says, "Paul Butterfield was literally the first person I saw when I got to Chicago to attend college. He was sitting on some steps, drinking beer and playing guitar." Bishop chose that school because of its proximity to the south side Chicago blues scene. Butterfield and Bishop got their first gig together in 1962, joined by Howlin' Wolf's rhythm section, drummer Sam Lay and bassist Jerome Arnold.

Sam Lay said, "If it hadn't been for Paul Butterfield the blues would never have gotten beyond the South Side. He not only opened the doors in Chicago, but also to the college kids. He introduced the entire country to the music." (Liner notes to *The Anthology* written by Tom Ellis III, released by Elektra.)

In 1965, Mike Bloomfield, another Chicago-born blues devotee, joined the band on guitar. They played the Newport Folk Festival that year along with an electrified Bob Dylan. Pete Seeger tried to take a fire ax to Dylan's amp cord but was restrained by cooler heads. Dylan got the headlines, but Butterfield's debut left the audience stunned and breathless. Most, if not all, had never heard electric blues before. Charles Sawyer (*The Arrival of B.B. King*/Doubleday), who has been working on a Butterfield biography, believes that were it not for Butterfield the blues would still be consigned to a niche audience instead of its current ubiquity.

Elektra released Butterfield's first album, *The Paul Butterfield Blues Band*, in 1965. The band's swagger and self-assurance were staggering. From the opening blast of "Born in Chicago," the record is a living thing writhing between your ears. The band included both Elvin Bishop and Mike Bloomfield along with Lay and Arnold.

Butterfield's singing and harp playing were electric. Butterfield sang in a strong tenor with generous range and a worldly-wise inflection that said this dude had been around the block. He knew the ropes.

Longtime blues guitarist and founding member of the White Trash Blues Band John Davis recalls Butterfield's electrifying debut at the Newport Folk Festival in 1965:

"I saw the Butterfield Band live on several occasions.

"The first time was quite memorable. It was at the Newport Folk Festival of 1965, the one where Dylan went electric, was booed, and where Pete Seeger pulled the plug on him.

"It was also the first time the band played with Mike Bloomfield. Anyway, the festival had a small blues stage, where Flinn and I saw all kinds of great blues players like Lightning Hopkins. At the end of the afternoon, up comes these sharp-looking white kids with their shades and sharkskin suits (the bass player and drummer were black dudes). It was shocking, not only because there were the first white people on stage, but also because they were the first there to play the Devil's invention, the electric guitar!

"From his first solo, Bloomfield was having an orgasm with every high note. Off to the side, I saw Alan Lomax, Jr., who, I believe, organized the show. He had a pained look on his face, i.e. it was sacrilege for white kids to be playing the black man's music. Standing nearby was Albert Grossman, the manager of Dylan, Janis Joplin, and The Butterfield Band. He was enjoying the show and the enthusiastic response of the audience. Suddenly, the stage went silent, except for the drums, as Lomax had pulled the plug on the band. Immediately, Grossman jumped Lomax, and I witnessed the hilarious sight of two middle-aged, fat guys rolling around in the dust, trying to hit each other. As I remember, the band was eventually plugged back in and allowed to finish one song, but that was it.

"That night (Sunday), Dylan had his historic show with the Butterfield band backing him up, but no Butterfield. The story I heard was that at rehearsal, Dylan had kicked Butterfield off the stage, telling him to come back when he learned how to play the harmonica. I also heard that Dylan told Bloomfield not to play any of those cliché blues licks! Actually, Flinn and I didn't stay for that last concert. We were so exhilarated by the Butterfield show that afternoon that we had little interest in seeing Bob Dylan. We got back into our 1954 Chevy and headed back to Madison.

"I believe the next time I saw the band was at a Chicago blues club called Johnny's. Their first album had come out by then and had caused a sensation with young, white blues fans. They were working on their *East-West* material, and probably were at their musical high point, with Bloomfield, Butterfield, and Bishop trading explosive solos.

"Later, The White Trash Blues Band opened for both The Butterfield Band and Bloomfield's new group, The Electric Flag (with Buddy Miles, who later played with Hendrix) at The Factory. I remember one after party at my girlfriend's house that Elvin Bishop showed up at. Another night, Bloomfield came back to my apartment, where all he wanted to hear was The Staple Singers (fortunately, I had several albums). He made a feeble attempt to pick up my ex-girlfriend, but was so drunk that he passed out in my bed."

Butterfield's second album, *East-West*, thrust a foot into jazz with the title track, a thirteen-minute blues/jazz safari that begins with Bloomfield's guitar vamping over a single chord for a dozen measures followed by Butterfield's harp. Sam Lay had quit the band and been replaced by Billy Davenport, a jazz drummer who encouraged Butter to explore extended forms outside the twelve-bar blues. "East-West" begins as raga, an Indian fugue that allows each soloist space in which to improvise.

As "East-West" builds to its first crescendo, a sitar seemingly enters in a modal drone. There was no sitar. "That was just Mike," says Elvin Bishop. "I think he was using an open string guitar, a Les Paul. Bloomfield was going for more of a Ravi Shankar feel. The way that song came about, 'East-West' as much as anything had its roots in blues clubs. It was an old tradition in the thirties and forties to have a shake dancer, some woman you wouldn't want to look at real close. Sometimes she had a snake. They'd play some semi-exotic song like 'Caravan.' If you listen to Jerome Arnold, you hear that dancer beat."

("Bloomfield would do a fire-eating trick. He'd soak a mallet in lighter fluid, light it and stick it in his mouth. As long as you keep blowing out you're all right.")

Bishop's and Bloomfield's long, sinuous lines intertwine like a double helix. Perhaps not as harmonically daring as *Bitches' Brew*, *East-West* nevertheless expresses a genuine jazz vibe. Having seen Butter several times I can attest that the band did indeed "change it up"—they never played the same solo twice. The piece holds your attention despite (or perhaps because of) the absence of clear-cut chord changes, and the mesmerizing quality of Bloomfield's and Bishop's guitars. *East-West* also contains a version of Cannonball Adderley's "Work Song."

The Butterfield Band was about to undergo big changes. Across the pond another musical adventurer set out on a similar journey.

CHAPTER 3
JOHN MAYALL
AND THE BLUES

John Mayall was born in 1933 in Macclesfield, Cheshire. John's father Murray was a jazz guitarist. John fell for the blues at an early age. After serving with the armed forces for three years in Korea he bought an electric guitar and taught himself to play guitar, keyboards, and harmonica.

In 1962, Mayall joined the Blues Syndicate, a jazz rock band formed by trumpeter John Rowlands and sax player Jack Massarik. Mayall is perhaps best known as one of the great explorers of talent, like drummer Art Blakey, whose Jazz Messengers served as a launching platform for countless jazz luminaries from Clifford Brown to Wynton Marsalis. Mayall's own band was called the Bluesbreakers and in 1965 he hired the Yardbirds' ex-guitar player Eric Clapton. Other Bluesbreakers included Peter Green, John Almond, Jack Bruce, Keef Hartley and Mick Taylor. In 1966, Mayall recorded *Bluesbreakers with Eric Clapton*, an instant classic. So far so good.

Mayall followed that release with the hard-edged and unsentimental *Crusade*. The record features Chris Mercer and Rip

Kant on reeds but they stick to the blues, drenching their songs in cerulean hues.

Mayall's epiphany occurred on his first visit to Los Angeles in 1967, and Laurel Canyon in particular, to which he moved in 1968. His exposure to the creative explosion had a profound effect on his music, which began to move away from 12-bar blues, most notably on *Bare Wires*. Mayall stayed with Frank Zappa for three weeks before returning to England. He moved to Laurel Canyon permanently later that year.

Bare Wires, the jazziest of Mayall's records, features the "Bare Wires Suite," a 23-minute opus encapsulating six movements using jazz tropes in the same way as Gershwin's *Rhapsody in Blue.* Both pieces use lush orchestration and blues-born chords to create music with one foot in jazz and one in blues. (The suite, or extended song cycle, will become a signature of jazz rock reaching its apotheosis on *Dreams.*)

"The Bare Wires Suite" begins with Mayall crooning over churchy organ, segues into "Where Did I Belong" accompanied by Henry Lowther's delicate violin. This section is pure blues although the arrangement and instrumentation are highly unusual with drummer Jon Hiseman already making himself heard via ominous drum rolls. "Start Walking" struts out the door over a bluesy vamp with a modal structure. Guitarist Mick Taylor enters with a fat tone before segueing into "Open a New Door," based on blues chords but rearranged, like many of the post-bebop era. Think Lee Morgan's "The Sidewinder" or most Horace Silver comps. Heckstall-Smith cuts loose with a rippling tenor solo that is pure jazz.

Mayall's slightly adenoidal vocals are spot on the melody. He doesn't bend notes or scat but that metallic edge to his voice makes him a compelling singer. The next section, "Fire," is free-form jazz with drummer Hiseman all over the place invoking both Blakey and Elvin Jones.

Right after *Bare Wires* Mayall sent the horns packing and reformed as a quartet with Mick Taylor on guitar, Stephen Thompson on bass and Colin Allen on drums. The graphics for

Blues From Laurel Canyon are amusing in hindsight with the longhaired and billygoated Mayall cavorting amid natural splendor like a satyr or a wood nymph. There are jazz overtones to *Laurel Canyon*, but nothing to match the unhinged ambition of *Bare Wires*. On "2401" Mayall plays harp like a sax. Of course it could be any instrument but the tone and changes are clearly reed like.

CHAPTER 4
SONS OF THE
BLUES PROJECT

Guitarist Danny Kalb formed The Blues Project in Greenwich Village in 1965. Initially the band included Kalb, guitarist Steve Katz, Andy Kulberg on bass and flute, Roy Blumenfeld on drums and Tommy Flanders on vocals. They acquired keyboard player Al Kooper at a failed audition for Columbia. Their first album, *Live at the Café Au Go Go*, was a success and led to early comparisons with the Grateful Dead.

The Al Kooper song "Wake Me Shake Me" from *Projections* is typical of the band's bluesy jams. You can hear the young Kooper straining to project his pitchy voice over the surging rhythm section nailed down by Kulberg's monstrous bass. The five-minute track allows each musician to stretch with technically modest but crowd-pleasing solos and features the loud/soft/loud dynamics that Kooper perfected on BS&T: *Child Is Father to the Man*.

Their second album contained an eleven-minute workout of "Two Trains Running" allowing the players to solo extensively.

Kooper's and Katz' desire to add horns to the band led to the break-up. In a nutshell, Kooper and Katz quit to form Blood,

Sweat & Tears, and Kulberg and Blumenfeld created Seatrain. Kooper went to LA followed shortly by Kulberg and Blumenfeld who felt they were missing out on the West Coast scene.

Kulberg and Blumenfeld drafted violinist Richard Greene, guitarist John Gregory, and sax player Donald Kretmar. They also acquired a lyricist, James T. Roberts. (Greene recalls, "Jim Roberts was there from the very beginning and he got laid a lot with his drunken poet persona.")

Greene proved to be the strongest voice and the greatest continuity between *Sea Train* and *Seatrain*, their follow-up. While *Seatrain* is a great rock record, starting with a twanging version of Lowell George's "I'm Willin'," it's their first record *Sea Train* that interests us.

With its ethereal arrangements and unusual instrumentation *Sea Train* instantly hooks you. The title track features sax, violin and guitar forming a silky front line. Elfin glades and rain forest ferns grow between Kulberg's bass and Greene's violin as the calm before the storm before the horns kick in. This was some head theater for someone listening on headphones while tripping in 1968. "With your fan, my fire turns to wind—Your glass fills mine with sand, You shout, 'I'm not your land!' And I hear the ground." Greene commands a chamber music interlude before the sax comes stonkin' back. (Greene recalls, "The solo in the song 'Sea Train' is me on Electric Violin—NOT GUITAR, we never had a guitar player who could solo for shit—except for Elliot Randall briefly.") Violin, sax and guitar glide through a rondo of delicate chamber music before flexing dynamically back to full band intensity.

"Pudding Street" explores Kulberg's flute tone in another piece of delicate pop chamber music that recalls the Zombies and MJQ pianist John Lewis' solo efforts. This would be a natural for Herbie Mann. Greene's violin solo encapsulates Seatrain's dynamics. ("I was very jazz influenced here.") They never fail to sustain interest through ingenious use of time and chord changes.

Intertwining guitar, electric violin and a set of descending chromatic chords etch "Portrait of the Lady" in crystal. Like all great pop—masters, Sea Train shift constantly from minor to major keys and back again.

Greene tells how he came to be in the band. "I was with the Jim Kweskin Jug Band. A man named Bennett Glotzer approached me. He told me he'd been asked by the band to 'find us a violin player.' So I went in and played with Andy Kulberg, Roy Blumenfeld and John Gregory. We worked the songs up in rehearsal. Andy would bang out the songs in a very crude form and we would work it over as a band—extensively. I was obsessed with learning jazz at the time—Charlie Parker, John Coltrane, Cannonball Adderley and Jean Luc Ponty."Recording the first album, everything I did was improvised. In that sense it was very much jazz. We did take after take. We would record rhythm tracks and overdub solos, except sometimes everything was done live—all at once, no overdubs, i.e. 'The Orange Blossom Special.'"

Greene went on to record albums with Red Allen, Bill Monroe, Gary Burton, The Jim Kweskin Jug Band, Melissa Manchester, Linda Ronstadt, Peter Ivers, Herbie Hancock, Paul Siebel, Ramblin' Jack Elliot, Andreas Vollenweider, Steve Wynn, The Blasters, Maria Muldaur, Geoff Muldaur, David Grisman, The Blues Project, James Taylor, Tony Rice, Emmylou Harris, Bob Seger, Brian Wilson, George Strait, Loggins & Messina, Crosby-Stills & Nash, Peter Rowan, Rod Stewart, Lacy J. Dalton, Jerry Garcia, Van Dyke Parks, Bruce Springsteen, The Brothers Barton, Tony Trischka, Sting, Joss Stone, Richard Thompson, Mandy Moore, Jennifer Leitham, Dan Hicks and "quite a few Bluegrass containing some jazz solo albums under my leadership, including three CDs of my Jazz String Quartet, the Greene String Quartet."

With the departure of all original members save Kulberg, Greene, and Roberts, the group reinvented itself as Seatrain and hired George Martin to produce their next two albums. *Seatrain* is a great rock record but the jazz is gone. Still one of my favorite records. This is Seatrain's "Jewish" record as opposed to *Marblehead Messenger*, their "Christian" record. *Seatrain* contains the Old Testament "Song of Job" and the Passover-like "13 Questions." *Marblehead Messenger* contains "Gramercy," "Protestant Preacher," and "How Sweet Thy Song." Greene adds, "Jewish and Christian records with an atheist violinist!"

Kooper put together Blood, Sweat & Tears in 1967 (www.bloodsweatandtears. com), taking Katz with him. Kooper's desire to add horns to the band may have led to the split. Initially, it was just Kooper, Colomby, Katz, and Jim Fielder. Shortly they were joined by alto player Fred Lipsius, who brought in trumpeters Jerry Weiss and Randy Brecker and trombonist Dick Halligan.

In an interview for *Drummerworld*, conducted by Jeremiah Rickert: (http://www.drummerworld.com/drummers/Bobby_Colomby.html),

Colomby said, "Steve Katz and I were close friends. His tenure with the Blues Project (band) was coming to an end and we decided to put a band together. At the same time, Al Kooper, who had already acrimoniously left the Blues Project, asked me to play with him to raise funds so he could move to England and produce records. I suggested to Kooper that he ask Steve to play on this occasion. He vehemently protested since he and Steve had a deep disdain for each other. I proposed the notion that by asking him to play, he could defuse the existing negative feelings. After making sure Steve wouldn't turn him down, he agreed and Steve joined us for the one time only show at the Cafe Au Go Go, in New York's Greenwich Village.

"Along with Steve, Al had asked Jimmy Fielder, a bass player he had recently heard in California. We played some of Al's newer tunes: "My Days Are Numbered," "I Can't Quit Her" and " I Love You More Than You'll Ever Know" (I thought it sounded an awful lot like James Brown's "It's A Man's World"). If my memory serves me, also on the bill was Paul Simon and Judy Collins. Despite the all-star cast, the gig barely raised enough money for milk shakes for the musicians.

"I asked Steve to ask Al if we could use some of his material in a band we were going to start. While in Washington DC with

Odetta, I received a call from Steve telling me that not only did Al agree that we could use his songs ... BUT that Steve asked Al to join the band as its lead singer. AND that we had a gig at the Village Theater (which later became the Fillmore East) as the opening act for the James Cotton Blues band AND (as if that wasn't enough information for one phone call) our name was to be 'Blood Sweat and Tears,' a name Al came up with while he accepted the invitation to play the gig. Colomby's version of this story was: Al was on the phone with the promoter while gazing at a Johnny Cash album cover. The album was called, Blood Sweat & Tears." (Al's version found in his autobiography, *Backstage Passes and Backstabbing Bastards*, has Al naming the band after his own bloodied fingers following an intense performance.)

"My origins as a drummer were steeped in jazz," Colomby continues. "Most of the musicians I hung out with were jazz musicians. However, most of my friends socially were rock or folk musicians. As a result, Steve and I developed the direction of the band by virtue of our individual influences. Al's great contribution, was hyperbole. He convinced not only record companies that we were the Second Coming, but rock writers and fans. He started a street buzz that was unbelievable."

John Simon produced the first record, *Child is Father to the Man*. It was an exciting brew of rock, jazz, psychedelia and folk and Kooper was a dynamic composer and arranger. However in the course of making the record he alienated several band mates with his high-handed manner. He also tacked a peculiar "Overture" on as the first track, effectively cutting the band off from their record. The rest of the record more than makes up for it (I've always liked the "Overture").

Kooper says, "I had a strong jazz period from 1960 to '64, learned and listened, went to a lot of shows. I have strong influences."

"I Love You More Than You'll Ever Know" starts the disc in typically strong fashion with this Kooper-penned R&B scorcher in tribute to Otis Redding, who had just died in a plane crash. (Kooper friend and future collaborator Mike Bloomfield also took Redding's death as inspiration for his band The Electric Flag.)

Katz introduces the song on guitar with his characteristic fat fuzztones. Kooper is well within his range as he croons the verse. The first time the horns chime in sends a chill up your spine. This is jazz rock's moment—the moment the horns chime in. The song has a solid bridge and hook, moving deftly from minor to major and back. Seminal moment when Kooper sings, "I could be president of General Motors, baby," and grunts in disgust. Lipsius' (over-dubbed) alto solo stands out.

The rest of the band had misgivings about Kooper's vocals and when they started to record, he sang the lyrics in French to loosen everybody up.

"Morning Glory" is notable for the introductory and closing fanfares and Kooper's churchy organ. Lipsius' horn charts are rich and inventive. Katz' vocals are adequate.

"My Days Are Numbered" is another Kooper R&B sizzler favored with a typically strong Lipsius horn chart and Jim Fielder's booming elastic bass.

"Without Her" is a Harry Nilsson comp with a hint of Brasil '66 in the piano guitar interplay. Randy Brecker solos on flugelhorn (channeling Herb Alpert), but nothing on this record suggests what was to come. For one thing, this BS&T album was the most tightly controlled of all. Kooper had the songs and often the arrangements down cold when the musicians showed up. There were no blowing sessions to work out arrangements. Brecker later cited this as one of the reasons he left.

No song captures the band's early magic better than Randy Newman's "Just One Smile," which Kooper gives the full simmering soul treatment. Cathedral-like horn charts frame Kooper's painfully raw vocals. The middle section consists of a haunting fugue among Kooper's organ, John Simon's organ and Steve Katz' lute. The horns snatch you up and sweep you along like a hundred footer at Waimea Bay.

"I Can't Quit Her," another great Kooper R&B smoker. Katz' "Meagan's Gypsy Eyes" is psychedelic folk with what sounds like a synthesizer. "Something' Goin' On" is a blues potboiler and the only place on the record where the instrumentalists get to stretch. Kooper's call and response with Lipsius is memorable.

"House in the Country" mixes a little Flying Burritos and Byrds sensibility with choogling horns. All the animal noises were created by members of the band in the only unsupervised free improv on the album. "The Modern Adventures of Plato, Diogenes and Freud" is a pretentious little slice of chamber rock heaven with a full string section.

Finally, "So Much Love" is yet another winner from Gerry Goffin and Carole King whose compositions would continue to appear on future BS&T records. *Child is Father to the Man* is an exhilarating yet frustrating experience. The band's potential is all over these tracks, held in check by Kooper's limited vocals. Kooper's vision and songwriting are galvanizing and prescient. One can only imagine what would have happened if he'd remained with the band and agreed to cede the lead singer position to someone else. These are still great songs. Why does nobody sing them? (Stop the presses! Larry Braggs sings "I Love You More Than You'll Ever Know" on *Sacred Ground*, California Transit Authority's second album. But more on this later.)

The record charted modestly and the band, led by Colomby, booted Kooper. Again from *Drummerworld*: "It should be noted that our first album was a commercial flop. Around 40,000 records had been sold. I admit to initiating the movement that eventually led to the ousting of Kooper. I felt we needed a voice that was distinctive, powerful. I felt Al could still contribute but not as lead singer." Colomby and Kooper remain bitter enemies to this day.

Kooper himself says, "The reason I was asked to leave the band was repertoire & arrangement differences. As it turned out, it was for the best because I violently disagreed with choices like 'Spinning Wheel,' 'Lucretia MacEvil' and their arrangement of 'God Bless The Child,' to name but three. However they were tremendously successful and award-winning with these choices.

In hindsight, I'd say Chicago was the better more tasteful and original band and the only BS&T album in *Rolling Stones* Top 500 is the one I was on. I don't think they are in The R&R Hall of Fame, but neither am I and they certainly didn't play much rock n roll. The band Chase was good, too.

"I think BS&T Chapter 2 alienated the original followers and gained the 'top-tenners' who were never really quality mavens. Chicago eventually went top ten, but not as unabashedly as BS&T. When the soul went out of the genre, no one wanted to ever revive what it became. I still play jazz rock tunes and my fans love it because I never betrayed them. Nina Simone told me once that BS&T's version of 'God Bless The Child' was 'sacrilege.'"

Brecker left to join Horace Silver where he was eventually joined by brother Michael on tenor. "BS&T was a very structured situation. I needed to stretch out and play." (randybrecker.com)

Child barely scraped the Billboard Top 50 and failed to produce a hit, but remains a favorite of college and progressive radio stations.

The band immediately set about finding a lead singer. They auditioned Laura Nyro and considered Stephen Stills. Judy Collins told them about beefy Canadian belter David Clayton-Thomas at Steve Paul's Scene in the village. (The Scene would prove to be a launching pad for more than one jazz rocker.)

"Every time the singer sang I just looked up at the stage and said, 'Is that voice coming from that guy?'" Colomby recalls.

"Out comes this magnificent voice that I thought matched the power of the horn section. To me that was always essential. It had to be a very compatible sound. He knocked us flat on the first verse of that tune. We knew we had found our singer." (Hank Borowitz liner notes to *Blood, Sweat & Tears* reissue, 2000.)

"My origins as a drummer were steeped in jazz," Colomby says. "Blood Sweat & Tears came into existence and defined a new category in popular music: Jazz/Rock. It was never embraced by critics as a pure art form but rather a hybrid. We also weren't considered either a sixties or a seventies band because our success came between decades. As a result, we are usually dismissed as an anomaly."

Under producer James William Guercio the group reformed with guitarist Katz, singer Clayton-Thomas, trumpet players Lew Soloff and Chuck Winfield, 'bone player Jerry Hyman, keyboard player Dick Halligan, Jim Fielder on bass and drummer Colomby. The original band members had disliked the "Overture" Kooper used as the first track on *Child*, but borrowed a page from his book by starting the new, eponymous record with Eric Satie's "Variations on a Theme." How toney can you get? Guercio did this partly to lull the listener into a sense of serenity so the band can smack him upside the head with the opening blast of "Smiling Phases." But really, who was fooled by this ancient tactic?

The Satie creeps in on little cat feet but soon the horn section is chomping at the bit. The opening fanfare of "Smiling Phases" makes clear there will be no more blackface. It's a smooth and enticing debut with sassy contrapuntal horn charts, Colomby's propulsive and musical drumming and Dick Halligan adding jazzy right hand that suggests a young Herbie Hancock. The horns square off with the bass before solemnly ogling an elegiac section that leads back to the fanfare.

Following the obligatory Steve Katz snoozer, the band kicks it up a notch with "More and More." Clayton-Thomas makes it sound so effortless—the wordless exhortations, the R&B tropes—he makes them his own. The band's version of Laura Nyro's "And When I Die" is an American masterpiece in the hoof prints of Ferde Grofe and Aaron Copland. A mournful harmonica sets the stage—an old cowboy perhaps, sitting around the campfire at the end of the day serenading the longhorns. Hop-a-long bass and drums underscore Clayton-Thomas' plaintive *cri de coeur*, which gathers steam until he is shouting at the devil. Dick Halligan's piano fills the bridge with saloon echoes. The song stops and starts, alternates between loping and full gallop, brakes for a horn interlude over the rhythm section's witty clop-clop before Clayton-Thomas takes it out. Come back Shane!

Who can forget this lyric? "I swear there ain't no heaven, but I pray there ain't no hell."

"God Bless the Child" is perhaps BS&T's best known single, Billy Holiday's ironic song and treatment turned into a full-court stomper. Clayton-Thomas' vocal is more soulful than Lady Day's, because Lady Day was not a soul singer. She was a wry observer. Sultry organ leads into two choruses of Clayton-Thomas mournfully singing the head before the bridge briefly suggests the storm to come. The piano leaps into little ostinatos, the horn section blows mellifluous raspberries followed by 'bone, trumpet, and sax solos that would be at home on a Woody Herman record. Nor does Clayton-Thomas sound foolish interjecting, "Wait a minute, children!"

This arrangement proved so successful that Canadian jazz phenom Nikki Yanofsky uses it almost note for note on her record *Nikki*, which she released at age sixteen.

"Spinning Wheel" is the singer's contribution and is notable for a very Harry James-like trumpet solo by Lew Soloff. The oompah horn section followed by the flute ostinato suggests a small town carnival. Perhaps Clayton-Thomas had a merry-go-round in mind.

Colomby takes a well-deserved spotlight toward the end of "Blues—Part II," an all-purpose blues jam designed to show off the soloists. Colomby is a highly tonal yet funky player who sounds a little like Philly Joe Jones. Eight minutes in bass player Fielder quotes Jack Bruce from "Sunshine of Your Love" from Cream's *Disraeli Gears*. The horn section jumps all over it before Katz quotes "Spoonful." The fanfare leading into the vocal could have come straight from the first album's "Something Goin' On." Clayton-Thomas sings, "You've made me so very happy," which comes from Kooper's "So Much Love" from *Child*.

Once again aping the first record, the album ends with a reprise of Satie. This record, probably more than *Child*, is a heavenly host of jazz rock. BS&T were to undergo many more changes. (Joe Henderson joined the band briefly: http://www.rdrop.com/users/rickert/bst-pg3.html)

"The month following Woodstock they began working on their next album. Before the album was released, they had to make a goodwill tour to East Europe, because Clayton-Thomas who was a Canadian citizen didn't have a green card. The members didn't like the idea of making a goodwill tour for the Nixon-administration but they had no choice if they wanted to keep Clayton-Thomas in the band. The tour was a major disaster. On the first night, in Bucharest, the young Romanian audience jumped to its feet and shouted "USA." The police responded by loosing attack German shepherds on the audience. The communist government gave orders to BS&T, 'more jazz ... less rhythm.'"
(http://www.classicbands.com/bst.html)
(www.bloodsweatandtears.com)

CHAPTER 5
BLUE-EYED SOUL

The Rascals are among the most successful blue-eyed soul acts—hell, pop acts in history. Their numerous top ten hits include "Mustang Sally," "In the Midnight Hour," "I've Been Lonely Too Long," "Groovin'," "A Girl Like You," "How Can I Be Sure," and the anthemic "People Got to be Free," which Eddie and Felix wrote in response to the assassinations of RFK and MLK. ("Ray of Hope" was written to honor Teddy Kennedy.) Hailing from Garfield, New Jersey, the Rascals included Felix Cavaliere, Eddie Brigati, drummer Dino Danelli, and guitarist Gene Cornish.

They were always the Rascals. When Atlantic signed them, a group called the Harmonica Rascals complained so the band changed its name to The Young Rascals, dropping the "young" after the Harmonica Rascals packed it in. At first they sang soul standards like "Mustang Sally," but soon Brigati and Cavaliere began to collaborate on more adventuresome material such as "Groovin'." The Summer of Love must have hit Felix like a tidal wave. Before you knew it he'd tossed his starched collar shirts for love beads and grown a beard. He looked like a smiling Charles Manson.

At his mother's urging Felix studied piano from age six to age fourteen. He got his start as a back-up musician with Joey Dee and the Starlighters and in 1965 formed the Rascals. Initially Brigati handled most of the vocals but as Cavaliere began to contribute more material, he sang lead on songs inspired by Ray Charles and other soul greats. Once Felix started singing, Brigati faded into the background. Cavaliere has a melodic croak that he himself likened to a bullfrog. Those vocal rough edges, which would look like a hairy caterpillar if you did a sine graph, hooked listeners through the gills. Texture wise, Felix is the opposite of the *bel canto* favored by white pop stars such as Pat Boone. Felix' voice is a file—a number ten rasp that scrapes flesh as it slides by.

This, coupled with a sure sense of melody and experimentation led Felix inexorably toward jazz. The change becomes noticeable on *Freedom Suite* (March, '69), a double record. The chrome double LP jacket was something to behold. (One huge argument for vinyl: record jackets. You can read them, try to figure out the pictures, or roll a joint on the album liner.) Songs such as "Island of Love," "Look Around," and "A Ray of Hope" not only reflected Felix' social consciousness, they led the way out of blues chords toward a more emancipated but hook-heavy sound.

"People Got to be Free" has a terrific horn bridge. Brigati and Cavaliere co-wrote "People Got to be Free," "Island of Love," "Look Around," and "A Ray of Hope," to my mind their strongest singles ever. The new direction, which seems perfectly conventional in retrospect, may have alienated long-time Rascal fans who preferred the simpler blues-based or ballad material. These new songs are bursting with falsetto choruses and fresh ideas. The call and response on "Island of Love" and a hook the size of New Jersey should have garnered far more attention than it did. The horns march triumphantly through the bridge as the song switches up a key and fades to a crazily stuttering trumpet. It's still pop, but it's fresh pop. (Arif Mardin, Vice President of Atlantic at the time, arranged and conducted "People Got to be Free," "Island of Love," and "Heaven.")

Jazz emerges on *See*, their next-to-last album for Atlantic, particularly on the cut "Nubia" with Ron Carter on bass. Carter sets the tone with his walking bass leading into one of Felix' most exquisite melodies and achingly effective vocals. One can easily hear Betty Carter or Cassandra Wilson singing it. Hubert Laws' ethereal flute floats like a hummingbird as the song shifts gears into a chanted tribal outro that fades leaving only the barest flutter of Laws' behind.

Their last album for Atlantic was *Search and Nearness* (April, '71), notable mainly for Felix' "Ready for Love," a showcase for his impossibly emotive voice and one of his greatest hook-laden songs. Flute figures prominently here.

On *Peaceful World*, the first Rascals album for Columbia, Felix brought jazz to the fore, bringing in Hubert Laws, Joe Farrell, Pepper Adams, Alice Coltrane and Ron Carter among others. That's either Carter or Chuck Rainey punching holes in the earth's crust for "Happy Song." Buzzy Feiten takes a minimalist guitar solo that suggests jazz in its restraint and Felix brings it back to earth with a falsetto wail.

CHAPTER 6
CITY OF THE
BIG SHOULDERS

Chicago (www.chicagotheband.com) began in 1967 when drummer Danny Seraphine asked saxist Walter Parazaider and bass player Terry Kath to throw in with him on a band. Both Seraphine and Parazaider had been studying music at DePaul University. All three had been kicking around the Chicago scene for years playing in cover bands.

Their first manager hung them with the moniker The Big Thing, which they hated. It was their ultimate manager, James Guercio, who suggested the name Chicago Transit Authority. The group included Seraphine, Parazaider, Kath, Trombonist James Pankow, trumpeter Lee Loughnane, keyboardist Robert Lamm and bass player Peter Cetera. Cetera was the last to join the group, freeing Kath to play guitar whereupon he transformed himself into a monster.

Chicago Transit Authority and *Chicago* (*Chicago II*) are pure magic. Rarely has a band been able to catch so much lightning in two consecutive bottles. Both records were double album sets. Unfortunately commercial demands, bad decisions and infighting took their toll on the band's sense of purpose and song-writing ability and while they have remained popular to this day, nothing really compares to those first two sets.

The explanation, I think, lies in the way they recorded their first two records. They worked the songs out in endless blowing sessions in a house that Guercio rented for them in Los Angeles. In Pankow they had a skilled arranger.

According to Pankow, "From its inception this was always a rock 'n' roll band with a horn section. But unlike other entities our horn section was approached as a melodic voice with the vocals, as another lead voice in and around the lead vocal lines."

"The team effort that went into that first album was clearly winning, instrumentally and vocally. The approach with so much brass ensemble playing was really unique and revolutionary," Lamm says. "And the way we looked at the vocals was in no small way influenced by the Beatles. That was a major influence.'" (*Liner notes to Chicago Transit Authority reissue, 2002*, by David Wild.)

Drummer Seraphine writes in his autobiography, "Being confined to the house on Holly Drive gave the band the freedom to concentrate on writing compelling original material. It was a non-stop jam session where everyone built upon each other's ideas. We were pushing our art to a new level. The group was tighter than ever and the new originals sounded mind-blowing." (*Street Player: My Chicago Story* by Danny Seraphine, Wiley.)

Seraphine studied with jazz drummer Chuck Flores and cites Gene Krupa and Buddy Rich among his influences.

The mix of brass and woodwinds gives Chicago a richer sound than bands that featured only brass (Chase) or only woodwinds (If). The horns are original in ways other bands are not. Both Butterfield and Tower of Power have one foot in rhythm and blues so you always have a pretty good idea of the kinds of chords they'll choose. Not so with Chicago. Like the Sons of Champlin, the horns made their way outside genre guidelines and in doing so came up with something fresh.

Coming at a time when the overwhelming majority of rock was guitar-based, *Chicago Transit Authority* hit with the force of a thermonuclear bomb. The fist-pumping horns define the band from "Introduction," in which they describe the entire melodic arc. Chicago's horn charts are both logical and surprising.

Pankow's trombone, more than trumpet or sax, defines their sound. He has carved out the meatiest 'bone role in popular music since Glenn Miller. There's a descending figure in "Intro" that sounds briefly like a college marching band before Pankow steps up. Following the stirring fanfare and statement of theme the chords slip into minor mode and guitarist Terry Kath gracefully leaps into the hole. Seraphine solos with nods to Buddy Rich and the song blasts to a stop. More than most bands, Chicago knows how to end a song.

"Does Anybody Really Know What Time It Is?" begins with a long, jagged piano leading into the triumphant strut of the horns (in 5/4) and Robert Lamm's existential question. In recent appearances Chicago no longer grapples with the 5/4 signature.

From: (http://www.songfacts.com/detail.php?id=98030): "Chicago singer and keyboard player Robert Lamm wrote this song and sang lead. He explained in the *Chris Isaak Hour*: 'I was a teenager walking down the street in Brooklyn, New York where I grew up. I walked by a movie theater and there was an usher standing outside taking a cigarette break. I said to him, "Hey man, what time is it?" and he said, "Does anybody really know what time it is?" I remembered that when I was trying to write this sort of Beatle-esque shuffle and I just explore the idea of "Does anybody really know what time it is?"'"

Aside from being a great sunny day song, "Beginning" is notable for Pankow's sure-footed trombone work and *sui generis* charts. Sometimes you hear a 'bone and it sounds like the player is struggling for breath and ideas. Never with Pankow. The song dwindles down to some crazy cowbell and percussion trailing off into the bush like a disappearing safari.

"Questions 67 and 68" finds Kath plucking a pointilistic wild mouse ride around the horns' celebratory fanfare, Speedy Gonzalez running rings around an elephant parade. "Listen" begins on a long sustained guitar note that flutters to life

"Poem 58" begins with acoustic guitar. Kath switches to electric for a spiky solo that builds in intensity and is about as subtle as a sledgehammer but never lacks for ideas before the song switches gears to introduce the vocals against Kath's repeated descending figure.

"Free Form Guitar" is self-indulgent nonsense. "S. Carolina Purples" is straight-ahead blues notable for Kath's slippery guitar and Lamm quoting "I Am the Walrus." "I'm a Man," the only cover (Spencer Davis Group) features kitchen counter-top percussion and chop sticks on plates. "Someday" is the most overtly political song on the album, but it is couched in enough generalities that young listeners will have no idea that this refers to the riots at the 1968 Democratic Convention in Chicago. Killer song, killer hook. "Liberation" liberates Seraphine to propel the band through a heart-in-throat instrumental.

Both this and *Chicago II* were produced by James William Guercio, who would prove crucial to Blood, Sweat and Tears' triumphant 2nd album. Guercio liked horns. Later, he created the famous Caribou Ranch recording studio in Colorado.

Chicago II came out in 1969. The first half of this double album features a suite drawing on folk, doo wop, jazz and R&B. Although the name is not on the album it's called "Ballet for a Girl in Buchannon." (Columbia recently reissued this record and the new version features the "Ballet for a Girl in Buchannon.") One reason there are so many parts to the suite is that Columbia at the time granted a copyright to each separate movement. The more movements, the more they had to pay out in royalties. There were seven pieces to the suite, not counting the five songs that preceded it.

Columbia revised their policy because of the band and you can see the results in *Chicago V* with only ten tracks.

The first half of *Chicago II* has an epic sweep steeped in blues like *Rhapsody in Blue*. It has power pop dynamics, which are changes, the mixture of technique and inspiration, that keep you anticipating. Good dynamics bring you to your feet. There's a reason a hook is called a hook. Chicago achieves this by constantly shifting meter, key, and mode creating tension that demands release. And then they release it in glorious rainbows of horn.

The horns state the "Movin' In" theme with Lamm's soulful vocal evoking Michael McDonald. The horns swing into dance mode before launching Walter Parazaider's hilarious "outside" sax solo. Trumpet and 'bone follow in a more conventional mode. Chicago knows how to end a song with a sudden blast that tips you into "The Road." Like all great pop masters Chicago moves effortlessly from major to minor and back again. Who can listen to Peter Cetera wail, "Now please don't misunderstand my loneliness" and not feel a chill up your spine? Cetera sings in tandem with Kath's sinewy guitar like the Blue Angels streaking through your brain.

"Poem For the People" begins with a simply stated piano theme followed by *a cappella* horns, shifts to minor, Seraphine doubles down on drums and the three vocalists harmonize the ironic lyrics giving way to an elegant horn procession. Kath's guitar flashes by like a comet. The song glides to earth light as a feather on Pankow's trombone.

"In the Country" begins with Lamm's soulful vocal backed by Kath's and Cetera's exquisite harmonies. The three trade leads, each declaring "I do love you." The horn charts sound like they were written in stone and handed down from Moses. Kath tacks on a twangin' coda and the horns explode into a carnival ballet. Each song segues seamlessly into the next.

"Ballad for a Girl From Buchannon" begins with "So Much to Say." Seraphine hovers over "Much" like a brooding druid, ominous and threatening. "Anxiety's Moment" illustrates the power of the major/minor shift as the horns embark on a genteel chamber dance and the song flows into "Colour My World" like the Missouri into the Mississippi. A simple piano motif signals Kath's soulful vocal. Pankow, who wrote the song, explained that, "It's a small segment of a multi-movement piece on our second album that is basically a tribute to my first love. I had been listening to Bach—the Brandenburg Concertos, and they had all those arpeggiated melodies. I sat at a piano and started messing around with these arpeggios. That cycle of arpeggios became the foundation of the song." (http://www.songfacts.com/detail.php?id=3480)

"To Be Free" is a punchy horn-dominated instrumental and showcase for Seraphine's propulsive drumming leading into the triumphant "Now More Than Ever." And that's just the first half.

The pompous intro to "Fancy Colours" sets up that sweet moment of release when the band bursts into swing. Parazaider dances ahead on flute until Kath breaks out the fuzztone and the song puts on the brakes with blasts of jarring dissonance from the horns.

Keyboardist Lamm wrote "25 Or 6 to 4" while living in the Hollywood Hills. The title refers to the time he was up late trying to write a song about trying to write a song. "Waiting for the break of day, searching for something to say." Unquestionably the most exciting song ever written about writer's block and a favorite of college marching bands.

"A.M. Mourning" and "P.M. Mourning" are classically structured instrumentals, mostly a showcase for the horns. "It Better End Soon" finds the band in hortatory mode about the people dyin'. The 2nd movement features Parazaider's flute over a gentle vamp. The 3rd movement finds Kath emoting that "we got a raw deal—they're killing everybody—they're killing me and you...." Absurd commentary coming from multi-millionaire rock stars but there's no doubt they felt this way at the time. The band was in Los Angeles during the 1968 riots at the Democratic National Convention in Chicago.

Chicago was to take several surprising directions over the years.

CHAPTER 7
COLOSSEUM

After Mayall broke up his Bare Wires band, sax player Dick Heckstall-Smith, drummer Jon Hiseman and bassist Tony Reeves formed Colosseum with keyboard player Dave Greenslade and guitarist Jim Roche. Roche was almost immediately replaced by James Litherland. Colosseum incorporates so many different styles into their work yet they have a unique sound due in part to the line-up, partly to their propensity for chilly art rock in the manner of King Crimson or Emerson, Lake & Palmer. They're self-mockingly pompous in a Col. Blimp sort of way. But there's nothing silly about the music.

As the sole horn, Heckstall-Smith had plenty of room to stretch Colosseum's sound is bluesier than most jazz rock bands and their thick front line comes from sax, organ, guitar as opposed to three or four horns.

"Backwater Blues" from their first album could be any British blues band, at least until Heckstall-Smith enters with his instantly identifiable sound.

"Elegy" has a modern R&B vibe recalling other progressive English R&B acts like Kokomo with a soaring Heckstall-Smith solo on soprano sax.

Jack Bruce's "Rope Ladder to the Moon" has a dissonant melody only a mother could love. Once they get past the bridge Heckstall-Smith finds fertile ground.

"Take Me Back to Doomsday" begins with Greenslade's lilting chamber music piano. The band surges into Nordic waters with big, somber Viking chords launching spindrift flute rock.

"Ides of March" begins as the soundtrack to one of those toney historical HBO productions—*Rome*, perhaps. Hiseman fills every inch of space with thunderous arpeggios. A lot of Colosseum sounds like it could have been done by Genesis or Pink Floyd. That's not a knock—it shows how close Colosseum was to British art rock. A haunted harpsichord veers from the path, enter Litherland steaming and the band morphs to hard rock. Amidst the frenzy Heckstall-Smith reaches for the highest note he can. The waves subside and it's back to a stately and altogether suitable denouement for a very dignified piece.

"Jumping off the Sun" recalls Fairport Convention on a sugar high with Litherland's pompous Jack Bruce-ish vocal.

"Theme From an Imaginary Western" is truth in advertising. This does sound like the fanfare that might begin a sprawling Sergio Leone epic. Everything Colosseum does has an epic feel to it.

"Daughter of Time" finds Heckstall-Smith leading the funeral procession with a somber statement of the theme. Litherland enters with an operatic reading of the lyrics

"Walking in the Park" is Mayall-esque blues, Hiseman swinging like a sumbitch. Unlike the gasping emotionalism of, say, Son Seals, Litherland solos without peaks and valleys, just a steady progression of ideas. Hiseman tacks on a neat coda, stumbling artfully to a close.

"Backwater Blues" from their first album could be any English blues band.

James Litherland, who played guitar for Colosseum, formed Mogul Thrash in 1969 with drummer Bill Harrison, bassist John Wetton, Average White Band alumni Michael Rosen on brass and Roger ball on reeds, and saxophonist Malcolm Duncan. Brian

Auger produced their self-titled LP, an exhilarating slice of Brit jazz/rock that is actually more interesting than Colosseum. Bassist Wetton takes an unusually prominent role, up front and in your face. The horns sound looser and jazzier than in Colosseum and the band stretches out on mostly Litherland/Brown compositions. This is well worth owning if you can find a copy.

CHAPTER 8
IF

If and Colosseum arrived more or less simultaneously. If was the brainchild of producer Lew Futterman. Lew was an agent who represented sax player Dick Morrissey and guitarist Terry Smith, both of whom played in R&B singer J.J. Jackson's Greatest Little Soul Band in the Land, which Lew also managed.

Terry Smith recalls, "We were all in the J.J. band together. One day the manager played me and Dick some tapes he'd got of Blood, Sweat & Tears and Chicago and asked if we'd fancy forming our own band. He assured us it could be done. In any case, some of the stuff Dick and myself had been doing already was not far off that style." (Liner notes to *If Europe '72* by Chris Welch.)

The addition of Dave Quincy on alto made If a two-horn band without brass contributing to their unique sound. "Well we wanted to get away from the old jazz club format of playing everything in 4/4." (Liner notes, Europe '72.)

The line-up shifted from time to time but the following players all played on the first four albums: J. W. Hodkinson on lead vocals, Lionel Grigson on keyboards, Jim Richardson on electric bass, Dennis Elliott on drums, with Dave Quincy on alto and tenor saxes, Terry Smith on guitars, and Dick Morrissey on tenor and soprano saxes and flute. These guys were mostly jazz players. Naturally Quincy and Morrissey take a great deal of solo space. In terms of improv, there is nothing from Chicago or Blood, Sweat and Tears that can compare. American radio audiences might not have sat still for a five minute sax solo, never mind the Grateful Dead's endless indulgences. Not overly concerned with American airplay, If thought nothing of releasing five, six, and seven minute cuts.

Miles Davis paid them his highest compliment, growling, "They don't sound white." The band may have been inspired by Blood, Sweat & Tears and Chicago, but they had their own sound. Morrissey frequently led the charge on flute backed by a churning, supple rhythm section and sax. Many of their songs were in odd time signatures as they vowed to shun the predictability of 4/4.

"What Can a Friend Say" from their first album is a typical If song, that is, atypical and thrilling with a unique English vibe that they share with Colosseum. They don't sound white. And they don't sound American. Partly it's Hodkinson's metallic vocals. The band often sounds like a stripped-down version of the Kenny Clarke/Francy Bolland Big Band. Like Chicago on their first two albums If worked out their arrangements in endless rehearsals, sifting and winnowing for the perfect balance of structure and freedom. All these songs are on *Anthology 1970 – 72*. There's a lot more If out there for those who are interested.

"Friend" begins with fluttering flute over Smith's machinegun tracers against the velvet background of rhythm and horns. A descending horn chorus leads to a slow hinge-like isthmus in the middle of the song. Morrissey explodes with a sizzling Joe Henderson-channeled sax solo that cedes to Smith's fat guitar. Smith builds an elegant solo over a simple motif. Jazz depends on improvisational ability. No Ifs, ands, or buts, this is jazz rock. At just under seven minutes "Friend" isn't exactly AM friendly but it took to FM like a journalist to an open bar.

"What Did I Say About the Box Jack?" was named after what Lew Futterman said to Brother Jack MacDuff in the control booth. Morrissey gets into a heavy flute thing with breathy undertones, like Mayall's "Room to Move" harmonica solo. Hear the human bellows at work. Morrissey cedes to Smith, who fires starburst patterns with his Stratocaster before throttling back to a handful of resonant notes.

"I'm Reaching Out on All Sides" is in 7/4. Smith gives the wah-wah pedal a work-out as Morrissey and Quincy duel contrapuntally on sax. Morrissey exchanges sax for flute and lights up the sky while Quincy doubles up on reeds like Roland Kirk. Smith tortures one note deliciously for twenty seconds.

From the second album, *If 2*, comes "Sunday Sad," a tone poem for flute and Spanish guitar that explodes at five minutes into a joyous carnival bounce. Little big band indeed.

From *If 3* comes "Forgotten Roads" featuring a searing Smith who holds a note forever before firing off dazzling starbursts of sound. "Roads" has a Who/*Tommy* vibe, a touch of Broadway.

"Seldom Seen Sam" is their "House in the Country," only this is delta country. Mealing has that juke joint bounce in his piano solo. J.W. Hodkinson sounds like he doesn't need a mike—that he could just blast it out to 50,000 people in a stadium if he wished. In Terry Smith, If had a guitarist fully the equal of Terry Kath.

"Child of Storm," also from the third album, was inspired by a H. Rider Haggard story and has a "Jazz Messenger type of arrangement for soprano and tenor sax." Geeks take note—how often does jazz cross paths with Rider Haggard?

From *Live In Europe* comes "Your City is Falling." Horns and keyboard limn the theme as Hodkinson rocks the vocal. Mealing sets the tone with slippery, elliptical organ before Morrissey steps up on dazzlingly precise and propulsive soprano. To his everlasting credit he will not make you think of John Coltrane. The horn section delivers a quick combo. Dave Eliot takes four and the orchestra falls in for the second chorus.

"Dockland" has a *Les Mis*/Broadway feel to it in Hodkinson's impassioned vocals and Smith's typically fiery and lyrical guitar work.

"Sweet January" is a dreamy ballad, hushed drums advancing under cover of gossamer flute. Flute elbows aside the vocal followed by a sweet Dave Quincy tenor solo.

If Europe '72 is proof that these jazz rock guys weren't just blowing smoke, they were smokin'. These tracks were recorded live before European audiences. "Waterfall's" Irish folk chords are off the charts in their un-blues. A flute/tenor bridge launches Morrissey's extended flute solo that illuminates the night like a 200-watt firefly. Quincy comes in with a repeated rising motif on tenor that leads back to the head.

By '72, the band had reached the height of popularity in Europe. They likely would have continued if Morrissey hadn't become seriously ill on an American tour causing the band to break up. However, for some members, the dream was far from over.

"The Light Still Shines" finds Hodkinson and Morrissey on flute in tight formation. A simple blues-based motif by the horns leads into Mealing's Cedar Walton-like solo. Mealing's lyrical playfulness is appealing. Morrissey slices the smoke with a fluttering solo until Hodkinson picks up the vocal.

"Sector 17" is straight up jazz—in 11/7—something Art Blakey might have played. Smith builds a diamond hard guitar solo that dazzles with McLaughlin-like bursts and runs. Quincy solos in eastern mode building a Coltrane-ish ziggurat that climbs and climbs right up to the frenzied Albert Ayler safety valve. The song sets itself down slowly. Crowd goes crazy.

"Throw Myself to the Wind" smacks of English art rock and begins with Hodkinson and the horns in perfect synch as they paint the jagged melody. Quincy, Smith and Morrissey trade fours.

Hodkinson belts the urgent, jazzy "I Couldn't Write and Tell You" evoking David Clayton-Thomas at the upper end of his range. Morrissey's flute guides the band through a sylvan glade.

The terrain becomes more rugged as Morrissey vocalizes through his flute. Smith takes over leaving plenty of space. The more he plays the less space he leaves until he fractures into a million pointillist notes, initiates feedback and gushes forth a veritable Victoria Falls of rushing guitar.

"Your City is Falling" is hysterical agit-prop featuring Mealing fleet and elliptical on Hammond B3 followed by Morrissey in an Eastern mode on soprano sax. Twenty-one year old drummer Dennis Elliott sounds sharp in his brief break.

Finally there is "What Did I Say About the Box Jack?" the director's cut. It begins with Quincy on tenor and Morrissey on flute sketching the fast-paced melody before they engage in mellifluous dialogue. Morrissey hums along with himself through the flute evoking Herbie Mann, but Morrissey is too original to sound like anyone else for long. The band drops away save Morrissey and Smith who follows him like Champ Bailey on a running back. Smith starts carefully as is his wont but soon starts ripping off dazzling runs backed by Mealing's Farfisa chords. Smith has Bloomfield's sense of timing building to an unstoppable juggernaut of guitar power. Morrissey and Quincy reenter on soprano and tenor in tight formation with Smith. A spacey middle section has a Mingus feel to it as Morrissey channels Dolphy. Everything out but the rhythm section finds Mealing conducting Sunday morning come to Jesus gospel on his Hammond. Hodkinson starts singing in tandem with Smith and it's a delta blues. The horns sway soulfully. The band filters out leaving Smith to build a trajectory of controlled razor-sharp beauty with tremulous quavers and just like that the blues are gone! The horns restate the original theme as endorphins flood our systems.

CHAPTER 9
ELECTRIC FLAG

As Kooper departed BS&T, Michael Bloomfield quit Butterfield determined to head his own band. He'd been thinking about it a long time and summed up his philosophy: "The Electric Flag is an American Music Band. American music is not necessarily music directly from America. I think of it as the music you hear in the air, on the air, and in the streets; blues, soul, country, rock, religious music, traffic, crowds, street sounds and field sounds, the sound of people and silence."

Electric Flag was brilliant blues-based jazz rock. *A Long Time Coming*, their second record and the first to feature what they actually played is an essential part of any jazz rock library. It was called *A Long Time Coming* because it was in the works far longer than most studio albums of the time, due partly to demands placed on the band by the score for *The Trip* and partly by the band's personal problems.

In 1967, Bloomfield recruited keyboard player Barry Goldberg, singer Nick Gravenites and bassist Harvey Brooks. Harvey recounts the tale here: http://www.youtube.com/watch?v=KF_AdivAAKw&feature=player_embedded

Bloomfield got a deal with Columbia and rented a house in Mill Valley where the band could stay and rehearse. Bloomfield recruited the nineteen-year-old Buddy Miles from Wilson Pickett's band (When he realized what was happening Wilson chased Bloomfield from the theater with a pistol). "Wilson Pickett, James Brown, Otis Redding, those were our models," Brooks says.

But before they could get down to the business of recording their first album they received an offer they couldn't refuse. Peter Fonda wanted them to score *The Trip*, a Roger Corman film written by and starring Jack Nicholson. Dennis Hopper and Brooks were also in the film, for which they received, among other things, a pound of pot.

The soundtrack is very good as far as it goes, but it doesn't really represent the band. *A Long Time Comin'* was finally released in March, '68, stunning music aficionados but leaving the general public cold. From LBJ's opening remarks, *Comin'* is like no record you've ever heard. The three horns, Peter Strazza and Herbie Rich on reeds and Marcus Doubleday on trumpet, forge a unique sound that meshes well with Bloomfield's vivid bluesy guitar. Nick Gravenites' vocals are strong and emotive.

Harvey Brooks says, "Bloomfield saw the band as a blues R&B band with BB King, James Brown and Otis Redding as the main inspirations. As the band started to rehearse and evolve the horn players began to organically add the jazz element influenced by John Coltrane and Miles Davis.

"Jazz was not part of his original vision but he was alright with it as long as it stayed in the basic blues style. No extended chords or unnecessary chords. We did get into extended jams that were blues in nature with the horn solos adding a jazz feel. Buddy and I kept the rhythm solid but loose enough for the melodic rhythms of the soloists to create a sort of blues-jazz fusion."

The jacket design is a dizzy blend of red and purple with an archetypal hippie chick staring out surrounded by wailing band members. It still raises a psychedelic hackle today. The photograph of the band that originally appeared as the back cover is as iconic as anything by Buffalo Springfield or the Byrds—it has that kind of old-timey feel to it. This was the first integrated rock band if you discount Butterfield.

Howlin' Wolf's "Killing Floor" is a flag-waving story of its time about a guy who should have gone to Mexico to avoid the Vietnam war but stayed behind for a no-good woman. Movies have been made from less. The horns propel the melody like dragon boat paddlers, with sharp little strokes. Gravenites wails the verse releasing Bloomfield into the ionosphere like a cruise missile. The soaring bridge with Herbie Rich riding the cables is classic horn rock. And like Chicago, they know how to end a song.

"Groovin' is Easy" is a time capsule from the Summer of Love, a paean to tuning in, turning on and dropping out. Nick Gravenites sings to an uptight girl—sounds like he's trying to get in her pants. The horn section struts. Bloomfield launches spectacularly with a shimmering upper register figure as the horns swagger toward the next verse.

"Over-Lovin' You" is soul in the tradition of Otis Redding et al, but it has a harder, less-commercial edge. Buddy's tom-toms introduce a psychedelic interlude before the horns come chooglin' in. Buddy is an impassioned vocalist with plenty of grit and sounds effortless save when he's straining for effect as in an inarticulate howl of longing toward the end.

"She Should Have Just" has a bittersweet vibe due to the use of strings and the one/two harmony the horns hit against Gravenites' flatted vocal in the bridge. Not being a musician, I asked my friend Mark who is an airline pilot about that weird harmony.

"Usually one on the root and the harmonizer on the 5th. Sometimes if there are two singers one will go to the fourth to 'pull' the lead singer to the chord change. Remember that the 'tonic' (Primo, root, 1st). its 4th, 5th, and 'octave' (8th) are all perfect intervals and provide a strong sympathetic pull.

"In Jazz and non-western music, where Pythagoras is unknown (or ignored), all harmonic bets are off. Just look at the origins of jazz! Most western music is based on a 'tampered' form of Pythagoras' string theory, and therefore non-'just,' but close. Since the western ear is trained for sympathetic pitch, we have learned to listen for our trained 'perfect' sympathetic fourths, fifths, octaves and primos. That is why if you have a diva singing a root, and a second singer harmonizing on let's say the minor 3rd, it would sound awkward to us. However, when scat singers duo, they often pick off-perfect pitches to provide that great 'rub.'"

"Wine" is juke joint jive given unexpected heft by the horns and Bloomfield's sleek heavy solo.

"Texas" is a gray/blue groove of slow blues that cuts like a filet knife. "I just got in from Texas, babe, you didn't even know I was around ... And when you saw me on the street woman you looked at me like I was a Ringling Brothers clown." Bloomfield surrounds Gravenites' raw vocal with a maypole of barbed wire as the horns march mournfully.

"Sittin' In Circles" evokes its bittersweet theme in the classic refrain and the way Bloomfield's guitar flashes lightning from the pink cloud of strings and horns. The horns alternately swoon and strut for this monster slice of soul.

"You Don't Realize," dedicated to Steve Cropper and Otis Redding, does them proud with its simmering "Woe is me" song. Miles is underrated as a singer. He emotes with controlled anguish and never sounds like he's straining. He tosses off the odd "But wait a minute!" without sounding forced or mannered. Gravenites gravitas.

"Another Country" is the most ambitious song on the album and one aficionados point to as evidence that the Electric Flag wasn't just another blues band with horns. The fire sirens say this is as serious as an audit. The chorus and verse radiate a subtle menace as Gravenites recites a litany of alienation—you wake up one day and things have changed so drastically you find yourself in another country. Two and a half minutes in the song blows up into dissonance, random noise, and radio snippets. A string section plays a weird descending motif that would be at home in a Hitchcock movie.

"Country" descends into chaos to create the tension necessary for that sweet instant of release when Bloomfield begins plucking almost idly at his guitar as the rhythm section falls in. The plucking becomes intense and structured, finds the sweet spot in the chord, works it and returns to the tonic with focused urgency as the horns kick it along. At over eight minutes "Another Country" gives Bloomfield space to build a powerful statement. Steve Cropper and Otis Redding would have liked this one, too.

Bloomfield quit the band he'd created after eleven months due to exhaustion. He was also fighting a heroin and pill addiction, a fight he would eventually lose. Bloomfield was a trust-fund baby who had inherited two million dollars. Nineteen-year-old Buddy Miles became the leader of the band, which carried on for another year before dissolving.

CHAPTER 10
BUTTERFIELD 2.0

In 1967, following Bloomfield's departure Butterfield reformed the band with saxophonists David Sanborn and Gene Dinwiddie, bassist Bugsy Maugh, and drummer Phil Wilson. Elvin Bishop took over the guitar chair. The new band began to explore beyond the blues.

Butterfield's new sound debuted on *The Resurrection of Pigboy Crabshaw*, named after Elvin Bishop's alter ego. I saw them at the Factory in Madison, WI in 1968. The power of the horns pasted everybody to the back wall. Butterfield had his hair slicked back like a greaser and wore a leather vest over a long-sleeved white shirt.

The change is apparent on *Crabshaw*'s first song, "One More Heartache." Sharp drums and hand claps hook you before Butterfield opens his mouth and when he does the horns fall in like trained seals. Two verses of searing blue/gray vocals and Butter bites down hard on harp as the horns kick it up. This is propulsive, ass-shaking stuff. The BBB's blues were far removed from the lugubrious acoustic Delta style.

Everything fell into place with 1968's *In My Own Dream*, Butterfield's finest album and one that established the band as a leader in jazz rock. "In My Own Dream" shows that had he lived

Butterfield might have become a major American song writer. "Dream" begins with a fat plucked string leading into an acoustic section in which guitar and piano state the head. Butter nails the tensile vocal with a gospel backing chorus, Bishop's acoustic continues to pluck at the medulla oblongata all the way to the bridge outlined by piano, bass and drums. A held piano chord introduces David Sanborn's spine-tingling soprano, which unfolds with the logic of an orchid. A great sax solo right up there with Coltrane's "My Favorite Things," including a nod to Trane. The other horns jumping in send a chill down your spine.

Fortunately, a document of the band in performance is available. *The Butterfield Blues Band Live* was recorded at the Troubadour in Los Angeles, March 21 – 22, 1970. The 77-minute disc includes both sides of the double album. Curiously, although David Sanborn is pictured twice in the liner notes, he is absent from the recording, which features Gene Dinwiddie on soprano and alto, Trevor Lawrence on baritone, and Steve Madaio on trumpet. The sound quality is excellent.

Butterfield leads off "Everything Going to be Alright" with *a capella* harp tracing bluesy arabesques, which coalesce into a chomp down hard mind meld with the hand-clapping audience.

Dinwiddie contributes "Love Disease," a lively jump blues that frames Dinwiddie's tenor solo that flows like an eager raconteur, *My Dinner With Dexter Gordon*, an explosion of ideas. The rhythm section is deep in the pocket while the rest of the horns add a sassy, playful backing chorus.

Guitarist Rod Hicks contributes "The Boxer," an up-tempo love/hate song about a girl who should have been a boxer "because everything you do knocks me out." Dinwiddie shoots from the gate with four bars of cobalt tenor. Hicks is a less dense player than either Bishop or Butterfield and has a country twang in his playing, a touch of chicken scratching. The band drops out for George Davidson's Philly Joe Jones by way of Billy Cobham solo.

"Driftin' and Driftin'" is mid-tempo blues with the mournful sway of a weary USO band. Close your eyes you can see the young soldiers clasping their dates close. Butterfield sings the head with Trevor Lawrence providing counterpoint on baritone. Butterfield takes a long solo showcasing his dry, droll, sure-footed harp work, double-toning himself as Hicks floats along below. The band drops out leaving Butterfield alone as he seems to turn his back on the mike and wander off into the wings, but it's the only minute that isn't in your face and it's done on purpose. Just a lonely cowboy. Butterfield's slightly vocalized breath comes through as an undertone, he returns to his mike with urgency and the audience starts clapping along. Butter holds a note for six seconds, dives down for a blue chord. Comparisons with John Mayall's "Room to Move" are inevitable and favorable. When the band finally chimes in you feel like you and Paul have crossed "The Empty Quarter" together and dived into a blue pool in Aqaba. Then it's Walsh's turn, lyrical and attenuated leaving more space than his predecessors. Where Bloomfield would have struck each note like a carnival gong Walsh dances around the tonic, revealing it through omission. This fourteen minute odyssey leaves no blue stone unturned as Butterfield ratchets it up and howls an impossibly stratospheric note for an impossible time.

"Number Nine" is a get-on-board-or-get-run-over song with Butterfield's harp dancing over the churning bottom, Trevor Lawrence's insistent baritone reminding you to always look down. The harp becomes just another member of the horn section. Dinwiddie explodes upward like that mystery contrail off the coast of California with a touch of Dolphy and some gut-bucket. Lawrence's baritone bushwhacks across terrain usually limited to tenors and Butterfield leaps back in with a fluttering, rhythmic attack and grunting subsonics that sound like a runaway train.

"Born Under a Bad Sign" creeps up on you like a bad dream with ominous bass and Butterfield's insistently moaning harp. The horn section sucker punches you in the gut launching Butterfield's self-pitying lament. He buttonholes you like a crazy drunk, pouring out his bitterness while frisking your pockets.

"Get Together Again" has a tent-revival quality as the band claps hands and sings like an old style gospel choir. It's just Paul and electric piano, an irresistible tumbleweed of soul. "Old people tell me you've got to kill to be a man...." You can almost smell the sandalwood incense. Butterfield was just as effective solo as with a band. After the song dies and the audience leaps to its feet cheering the band comes back in for a short reprise.

Hicks' "So Far So Good" is a brassy flag waver and showcases Butterfield's vocal chops at their height. He could have crossed over into jazz or pop had he wanted. After call and response with the horn section Dinwiddie soars on soprano, at times both atonal and musical. The modal, mid-eastern type section suggests Dinwiddie may have been listening to Pharoah Sanders. Dinwiddie traverses a dream landscape with a hint of percussion and finds the modal middle, focuses on an increasingly urgent vamp, draws the rhythm section in behind him and Butterfield takes command on vocals.

In 1975 in Boston, I saw Gene Dinwiddie and Buzz Feiten in a band called Full Moon. The music was an exciting mix of blues and jazz. They put out a record that is no longer available. The *Full Moon* album from the Larsen/Feiten Band is not the same music.

Dinwiddie may or may not have passed away. Nobody knows. Butterfield died in 1987.

Great appreciation and film clip of Butterfield at: http://www.bluesforpeace.com/paul-butterfield.htm

CHAPTER 11
EARLY WINTER

Edgar Winter (www.edgarwinter.com) was born in 1946 in Beaumont, TX, two years after his guitarist brother Johnny. Edgar was a child prodigy. He studied ukulele, piano, guitar, bass, drums and saxophone. Edgar worshiped Hank Crawford and Cannonball Adderley. Both Johnny and Edgar are gifted musicians. Both are albino. But the most important thing about them is Edgar's voice.

Edgar sounds like a cat in heat at the very edge of hearable frequency yet awesomely in key and on time. Edgar's voice can raise the dead. The first time my Aunt Eleanor heard Edgar she dropped her teacup.

In 1968, Steve Paul, owner of New York's Scene (where David Clayton-Thomas was discovered) invited Johnny to perform. Johnny's band included Edgar on keys, Tommy Shannon on bass and John Turner on drums. Paul began to manage Winter and scored a recording deal with Columbia in 1969. Shortly thereafter Epic, a subsidiary of Columbia, signed Edgar. (Columbia/Epic had a soft spot for jazz rock, producing Chicago, Blood, Sweat and Tears, Edgar Winter, Chase, and Dreams.)

Most people know of Edgar, if they know him at all, for his #1 1972 instrumental hit, "Frankenstein." By then Edgar had left the horns and experimental writing behind for glam rock, which he navigated effortlessly with the assistance of longtime partner and singer/guitarist Rick Derringer ("Hang On Sloopy" by the McCoys).

Edgar released his first record, *Entrance*, in 1970. The first half consists of *Winter's Dream*, a seven-part suite that uses blues chords as a launching pad for a highly dramatic (some might say histrionic) and tuneful song cycle. As is so often the case, an artist's break-through work may represent the pinnacle of his career, and many artists never find a second act. Edgar has found many acts and continues to thrive, but none of his recorded output can match this initial burst of melodic invention.

"Entrance" begins with dreamy mallet and brush work as Edgar lays down the head on organ. The deceptively simple tune is one massive hook with a throbbing bass goosing it along. Edgar's straight-ahead vocal does nothing to prepare you for what is to come. "Entrance" almost has the feeling of a Renaissance chamber recital with its stately keyboards and processional feel. "Where Have You Gone" brings with it the chill of winter (no pun intended) in the sudden shift to minor key and Edgar's ominous warning jumping to falsetto for the refrain and as horns rise from the depths Edgar looses the Yowl. How does he not destroy his larynx? The Yowl commands your attention. If America's teachers had the Yowl, our children would all be Rhodes scholars. Yet in terms of Edgar's records, you ain't heard nothing yet.

"Rise to Fall" begins as a series of ascending arpeggios with a subtle rock kick and the elegant simplicity of John Lewis' *The Golden Striker*. "Come and see my church and my steeple thousands of people are praying.../Find the ark in your head in your heart in the garden where children are playing ... Don't refill my cup you can kill me and leave by the stairs in the rear." Jimmy Gillen's hushed drums perfectly counterweight Edgar's eerie voice. The spooky melody belongs in an Andrew Lloyd Webber show.

"Fire and Ice" is another killer blues-based song. Edgar hits the stratosphere for the second verse as the song sashays into a bluesy vamp delineated by Randal Dolanon's laconic guitar. Edgar launches into a sax solo that is merely a recitation of every technique he knows bereft of purpose, but really, the man's not perfect. It might be too much to ask that he be a brilliant composer, pianist and singer without demanding that he play the sax well. Actually, Edgar is a fine saxophonist, just not here.

The outro is as pleasing as the intro with an attenuated verse that slows to an elegant shuffle. The horns sound a fanfare and the piano takes us out into the rushing torrents of "Hung Up," another blues/rock cruise missile with your name on it. There is no chance of mistaking Edgar for someone else. Jimmy Gillen adds a neat little drum solo that leads into the strutting "Back in the Blues" with brother Johnny on harp. The lyrics sound like the Sphinx, Wes Studi's character from *Mystery Men*. Edgar's solo here is restrained and logical before the strings signal a return to "Re-Entrance."

The suite ends on a triumphant note with tympani, horns, strings, and a cast of thousands.

Edgar's Southern Gothic "Tobacco Road" features a gloriously overheated vocal. Edgar is a born raconteur—you can see him behind a pulpit raining down fire and brimstone on a mesmerized congregation. Listen to his sustained yowl at the end and look outside your windows. Count the cats.

"Peace Pipe" is a jazzy potboiler that lets Edgar play around with the echo feature on his alto.

In 1971, Edgar formed a new band with singer/sax player Jerry LaCroix whose raspy-voiced tenor nicely complemented Edgar's unique vocals. With Jon Smith on tenor and Mike McLellan on trumpet, they had a four-horn section. Guitarist Floyd Radford, bassist George Scheck and drummer Bobby Ramirez rounded out the band.

Their first record was *Edgar Winter's White Trash*.

Some reviewers have likened this band to the Stax/Volt sound. Certainly Edgar was drawing on a tradition of laid-back soul, blues, and church gospel in crafting this lively record. The air of Serious Intent that permeated *Entrance* has been replaced by a woozy, honkin' Saturday night vibe. "Give It Everything You Got" opens with the swagger of the Virginia State Marching Trojan Explosion taking the field at half time. Edgar and Jerry trade vocals before joining together in unholy harmony. Scheck carries the band for four measures of booming bass. Edgar's progress on alto is evident in his call and response with LaCroix.

"Fly Away" is slow rollin' Southern swamp rock with church chorus backing LaCroix' lead. You can hear Dr. John or Allen Toussaint playing this. "Where Would I Be" is barbecued power ballad. LaCroix is a strong vocalist in the David Clayton-Thomas mode. His tenor solo is just right. Edgar provides swooping, coyote harmony.

"Let's Get it On" is a come-on song with a multi-rhythmic intro and a sizzling Radford guitar solo. That's LaCroix on harp. "I've Got News For You" is she-done-me-wrong blues sung by LaCroix.

"Save the Planet" begins as ragtime piano Sunday morning, Brother Edgar at the keys. This perfect melding of Green Peace concerns and the church should be the anthem of the environmental movement. LaCroix sings the first verse and bridge with Edgar yowling. The song puts on the brakes with a full horn press as the choir reverently asks, "Will it be Mr. White ... mmmm ... will it be Mr. Black?" while Edgar performs breath-taking vocal maneuvers. Makes you want to hear him in a pure jazz setting. Edgar's closing duet with LaCroix crushes.

Edgar sings the gospel-hued "Dying to Live," and proves he's just as compelling within the normal human hearing range.

"Keep Playing That Rock and Roll" is signature for Edgar, as "That's Life" was for Sinatra and "Born to Run" for the Boss. This autobiographical rouser tells you all you need to know about the Winter esthetic. Beginning with barrelhouse piano, the horns kick in beneath Edgar's pellucid vocal. The horns roll in like waves buoying up the vocal, not taking lead as in Chicago, Dreams, or Chase. The point is Edgar was getting less jazzy.

Derringer takes the punchy guitar solo. He would become a major influence in steering Edgar to glam rock.

Edgar's voice makes even the turgid "You Were My Light" interesting.

"Good Morning Music" is mostly just Edgar and piano like Valerie Simpson's "I Don't Need No Help." They use the same chords. The bass and drums are superfluous at least until the song shifts into third gear and the cowbell and congas enter. Derringer delivers another concise slice of Midwestern power pop on guitar. I would love to hear Edgar do a solo album accompanying himself on piano. He appears to be more adventurous melodically when he's playing keyboards than when he's playing saxophone.

Road Work came out in '72, but I'm including here because it's so much of a piece of what has gone before. The big change on this live album is that Rick Derringer and Randy Hobbs have replaced Floyd Radford and George Scheck. There are two trumpeters, Mike McLellan and Tilly Lawrence. Sometimes Marshall Cyr replaces Tilly. LaCroix and Jon Smith play reeds. This is one of the first super groups, really, when you consider what Derringer brought to the table.

LaCroix introduces "Save the Planet" with a call for audience participation. These guys always sound like they're having a blast and so is the audience. When the horns line up for the fanfare at the bridge Edgar begins to circle the melody like a demented crow. You fear his voice is going to blow like an overloaded amp. It never does and he always comes in on key. LaCroix' scratchy voice provides the perfect foil, like a dog and a cat harmonizing. Winter and LaCroix engage in a contest to see who can sustain the longest buzzsaw note. Edgar wins on points.

"Jive, Jive, Jive" is a jump blues like you might hear any weekend in the delta. Jon Smith shows off his tenor chops.

"Can't Turn You Loose" is a credible stab at the Stax/Volt sound, especially Otis Redding. LaCroix delivers the grit convincingly.

With "Still Alive and Well" Rick Derringer kicks the door wide open and the band began to edge away from blues and jazz toward a rockier sound. Winter adopted an entirely new image for his next record, *They Only Come Out At Night*, which contained his only number one single, "Frankenstein," so-named because it was pieced together in the editing room from numerous recordings. Recently, Edgar has returned to jazz with his record *Jazzin' the Blues*.

(An unrelated side note: my friend Tim Truman is a comic book artist. In 1995, he and writer Joe Lansdale, who like the Winters hails from East Texas, wrote a Jonah Hex story called "The Autumns of our Discontent" in which two albino brothers named Johnny and Edgar were portrayed as whiskey-swilling murdering vermin. "Miffed that DC Comics portrayed them as 'vile, depraved, stupid, cowardly, subhuman individuals who engage in wanton acts of violence, murder and bestiality for pleasure and who should be killed,' the Winter brothers sued DC and the creators of *Jonah Hex: Riders of the Worm and Such* for appropriation of their names and likenesses under CA Civil Code section 3344." Ironically, both Truman and Lansdale are huge blues fans and fans of the Winters.

The suit ground on for years until the Supreme Court of California finally found in favor of the defendants on the grounds that the Autumn Brothers was parody protected by the First amendment. "Finally," Truman said, "I had to sell my last guitar to pay my legal fees."

CHAPTER 12
TOWER OF POWER

In 1968, Oakland sax player Emilio Castillo met baritone player Stephen "Doc" Kupka, when Doc came to audition in Emilio's kitchen. Emilio's father took him aside and said, "Hire that guy. He's got something." Tower of Power began gigging around Oakland in August, 1968. They have been at it ever since and have accumulated an outstanding book of soul originals that often edge into jazz, especially during live performance. Four original members, Castillo, Kupka, drummer David Garibaldi and trumpeter Mic Gillette remain with the band today. Unlike Chicago and Blood, Sweat and Tears they have never lost their soul or their mojo.

The five-man Tower of Power horns are much in demand from Linda Ronstadt to Aerosmith. TOP have produced twenty-three albums of mostly original material. Their swooning fanfares unfold like peacocks' tails. They usually begin their sets forty-five minutes late but the sound is perfect. You can be standing anywhere in front of them, inside or outside, and you hear each instrument and vocal distinctly and clearly. To see them in concert is to experience one of the tightest bands in existence. They swing, they pop and their enormous catalog includes plenty of space for soloists. Doc Kupka's baritone gives them an unmistakable signature sound. They've had lots of vocalists over the years. Their current lead singer Larry Braggs is one of the best.

In 1970, after several appearances at Bill Graham's Fillmore West, Tower of Power signed to Graham's San Francisco label and released their first album, *East Bay Grease*. *East Bay Grease* is murkier and looser than subsequent albums, which may simply have been a function of youthful rough edges. It contains only six songs beginning with "Knock Yourself Out." These songs sound more like riffs, and are mostly opportunities for tenorman Skip Mesquite and trumpet player Greg Adams. (Lennie Pickett took over as lead tenor on the next record and stayed with the group for many years before becoming musical director for *Saturday Night Live*.)

Following *Grease*, the band signed with Warner Brothers for whom they released six albums. To discuss every song on every album would require a book of its own. *Bump City*, their first record for WB, yielded the hit, "You're Still a Young Man." We'll consider two WB albums, *Back to Oakland* and *In the Slot*, their last for Warner Brothers.

Back to Oakland begins with a furious snippet of choogling horns called "Oakland Stroke," which fades out like a circus train and is notable for David Garibaldi's in-the-pocket swing and Mic Gillette's high-blippin' trumpet. "Don't Change Horses in the Middle of a Stream" begins with Chester Thompson's Jimmy Smith-like organ swells as singer Lenny Williams (who wrote the song) coolly leads the ensemble through this witty mid-tempo sizzler. Following two verses on the tonic the band changes down for the bridge. Bruce Conte lays in a slow but right-on-time guitar solo saying more with less.

"Just When We Start Makin' It" is a slow-cooked soul ballad with exquisite attention to detail like the brief cascade of horns at the start of the second verse. A female chorus backs Williams on the irresistibly sweet bridge. Thompson owns the latter third with his ostinato-happy Hammond B3.

Thompson's "Squib Cakes" is a blues-based jam session with room for everyone to stretch out. Garibaldi sets the pace with an addictive beat. Doc Kupka slides beneath with his honkin' baritone and the horn section joins in with mellifluous counterpoint to Thompson's organ swells. Conte solos on guitar parceling out thrifty notes like a man saving for a rainy day. Greg Adams' flugelhorn has no such problem. Lenny Pickett channels King Curtis for his tenor solo and Thompson brings up the tail with rippling organ. You would not be surprised to hear this at the Village Vanguard or Birdland. They resist the easy temptation of jamming over one chord. You can always count on TOP to deliver the bridge and the hook.

"Time Will Tell" is another swooningly gorgeous ballad by Kupka and Castillo, who write the bulk of the material. TOP has always been democratic about its songwriters, but Kupka and Castillo have got the chop. Their "I Got the Chop" is like a full-body massage—they hit every part of you with syncopated soul from head to toe. Listen to Doc's baritone goosing the ensemble. TOP are the most syncopated band in the world.

"Love's Been Gone So Long" is a showcase for Williams' bluer than blue note-bending voice.

"Below Us, All the City Nights" begins with a dazzling fanfare buoyed on a full string section as Williams croons the bittersweet melody. The chorus would melt a glacier. Talk about make-out music, this is right up there with Sinatra.

Finally, "...Oakland Stroke" fades in as if it had never stopped and then fades away.

In the Slot, with its pinball machine cover was TOP's last for Warner Brothers prior to jumping to Columbia. It was their seventh album in five years. Few songwriting teams have lasted as long and produced as much good material as Kupka and Castillo. Hubert Tubbs had taken over as lead singer.

"Just Enough and Too Much" works you over like Marvin Hagler with baritone thrusts and body blows to every human pleasure receptor. The hook is plunging into a hot steam bath after a hike through the snow. This is propulsive, booty-shakin' stuff. Conte has added some flash to his pared-down guitar solo, but not too much.

Lenny Pickett's tenor solo on the Bill Withers-like "Treat Me Like a Man" is spare and bracing. Tubs is a typically powerful TOP voice. "If I Play My Cards Right" is a droll make-out song, Kupka tugging at your sleeve with that baritone like a persistent child. Pickett channels Gene Ammons in his short, sweet tenor solo. "As Surely as I Stand Here" begins with a mini-fanfare before dissolving into a velvet ballad with female backing chorus. I'm yawning. But the song isn't for me, it's for young guys on the prowl. Women love this song.

To my mind, the record really begins with "Fanfare : Matanuska" and builds from there. TOP has created many dazzling fanfares over the years (one of the best is on their hard to find live '88 *Direct* album) and this is right up there, winding you up before launching you into "On the Serious Side," an irresistible slab of Hammond B3 and smearing horns that has a James Brown feel to it.

Garibaldi sets the funk into "Ebony Jam," an instrumental that the Bobby "Blue" Bland Band might have played prior to the singer's appearance. Pickett leads on tenor with a touch of King Curtis before he switches up to fractal fragments. Greg Adams blows some Freddie Hubbard-inspired flugelhorn. Chester Thompson holds one organ note for four measures before laying down a lilting bridge over which the horns dance, more mashed potato than foxtrot.

"You're So Wonderful, So Marvelous" has a Rascals-like melody and a fantastic bridge. Tubbs is Stax/Volt perfect and this song should have been a monster hit.

"Vuela Por Noche" is another jam with arpeggiated horns not unlike *Chicago II*. Another convincing argument why TOP is just as much jazz as rhythm and blues, this could have come off a Lee Morgan date. Thompson's flowing classical piano chops lead us into "The Soul of a Child," another swooning ballad with a bridge the size and shape of the Golden Gate. You can picture Sinatra singing this as the theme to a Disney movie. By the time

Tubbs reaches for that high note on "Where does it go?" there won't be a dry eye in the place.

"Drop It in the Slot" is as tart as "Por Noche" was sweet, a super-syncopated dance ditty that will have Aunt Eleanor shaking her ass. We will return to TOP following their switch to Columbia.

CHAPTER 13
DREAMS

Keyboard player Jeff Kent and bass player Doug Lubahn were two rock songwriters and friends of Stephen Stills. Stills' sometime drummer Dallas Taylor occupied Stills' Sag Harbor A-frame and invited Kent and Lubahn to stay with him. Kent says, "The place had a B3 organ, some Leslie speakers and a set of drums so we ended up playing continuously in this house, just jamming up material." (Liner notes to *Dreams* by Bill Milkowski, Columbia Jazz, 1992. This record was last released as an import in 1997 and is very hard to find. There's a 2010 import containing both their albums.)

Lubahn met trombone player Barry Rogers who was in an R&B outfit called Birdsong, headed by Edward Birdsong. The group included brothers Michael and Randy Brecker on sax and trumpet and drummer Billy Cobham. Barry persuaded Michael and Billy to join Jeff and Doug in some jam sessions and Dreams was born. John Abercrombie, fresh out of Berklee, became their lead guitarist. Randy joined, and Edward Vernon on lead vocals.

Randy Brecker writes, "Dreams' featured arrangements that were grown organically by rehearsing every day. Nothing was written out. The charts changed every night and grew with the band. Barry Rogers was really the heart of that band—his experience with Eddie Palmieri jamming up parts inspired Mike and I to rise to his level, so the horn 'parts' were amazing.

"BS&T's arrangements were great, too, but they were written by Fred Lipsius and we just played the parts he wrote for us. There was very little room to 'stretch out.' The Dreams' records still hold up—I listen to them all the time. Billy Cobham invented that style of drumming and it was a unique horn section and great tunes that were made to order for us to jam upon.

"As far as I know Doug and Jeff were a songwriting/singing duo—they met Barry Rogers who in turn involved Mike who had just moved to NYC. Then Mike suggested me and Billy Cobham since we had been recently laid off from Horace Silver, and we all in turn looked for a strong lead singer and came up with Eddie Vernon. After a few gigs we decided we needed a guitar player so we had 'auditions' and John Abercrombie and his wha-wha fit the bill. The idea was to jam up horn lines and keep it loose a la Mingus—which we did—nothing was ever written down. The tunes and arrangements evolved each and every night."

The resulting record and tour represents the apotheosis of the American jazz rock movement. In nineteen-year-old Philly native Michael Brecker they had a tenor player of unprecedented improvisational ability. His tenor is more often than not the lead instrument tracing masterful lines you'd swear were written down but they're not.

"Devil Lady," lopes in on Kent's piano and Randy's puckish trumpet peeps. The three man horn section has a very different sound than Chicago. The emphasis is on the tenor and trumpet, not the trombone and each smear of color snaps with sass and elasticity. You feel Cobham through your feet.

The horns on "15 Miles to Provo" command your attention via Randy's over-the-top bridge and tremolo, but it's not a very jazzy song, more of a country thing.

"The Maryanne" is a mournful ballad shuffling over long lines of trumpet and 'bone that evolves into chilly Nordic art rock.

"Holli Be Home" begins with oblique, questing trumpet setting the stage for the sweet release of the tonic and Vernon's attenuated vocal buoyed by the sunny horns that intertwine into a wail of dissonance before fading for the return of the main theme. Randy's fleet mute work blends seamlessly into the chorus.

"Try Me" was arranged by Michael and is a showcase for the telepathic horn section, an up-tempo rocker that Vernon delivers with urgency. Abercrombie's angular guitar shuns rock convention in pursuit of cosmic modality. The horns use that one/two harmony for a welcome touch of sour.

The "Dream Suite," written by Kent and Lubahn, begins with "Asset Stop," Michael wailing on tenor with a unique crying quality. No other rock band put the sax out front to lead the parade, not like this. The suite is a juggernaut of joy, a triumphant tour of the American song style from Cole Porter to the blues. Mike begins on unaccompanied tenor assessing a series of filigrees that coalesce into a bluesy figure. The rhythm section falls in behind him and Mike struts like a cheerleader tossing his line high into the air and catching it unerringly. The refrain with Randy's fluttering trumpet is like some East European Gypsy Carnival dancing into town. Squawking horns and drums carry forward briefly before the rest of the band joins in. It spins off like a Rube Goldberg invention, dissolves into a series of competing horn riffs.

The horns assume a boozy swagger, slow way down and come back as the stage band in a Berlin cabaret ca. 1932. A chamber music interlude lays carpet for the painful opening trumpet blast of "Jane," a slice of Brechtian musical theater with a killer hook and chorus. The horns take lead and have all the good lines. "Jane" dissolves into a fading calliope organ vamp, which disappears around the corner and returns as throbbing bass over which Abercrombie fizzes like a mad scientist with a new toy. The wry, bluesy horns are the antithesis of Chicago's lyrical braggadocio.

Mike's tenor solo on "Crunchy Grenola" ripples and flows like a mountain river in May. Everyone drops out but Cobham, letting Mike solo for four measures leading into the triumphant chorus that flows endlessly by like a cascading river. Cobham breaks free with drum roll, the band pivots into studied dissonance and fades away leaving Cobham to deliver. This is the drum solo against which all other drum solos are judged. He starts off in bebop and finishes in funk.

"New York" is as iconic as Bud Powell's "Parisian Thoroughfare" and in the same way: its ability to conjure and summarize the mood of a city. This "New York" is a throbbing, soulful evocation of the city that "moves too fast" with Randy's trumpet tumbling high above the ground without a net. "Slow down ... New York City ... you move too fast." His trumpet has an organic human quality.

Dreams put out a second album but it wasn't as strong. Soon Randy had rejoined the Horace Silver Group along with his brother Mike. (Check out *In Pursuit of the 27th Man* on Blue Note.)

CHAPTER 14
CHASE

Bill Chase grew up in Boston. His father played trumpet in a marching band. While attending Berklee School of Music in Boston Bill saw the Stan Kenton Orchestra featuring Maynard Ferguson and decided that he wanted to be a jazz trumpet player. Chase played with Ferguson, Kenton, and Woody Herman. Chase was freelancing in Las Vegas when the Beatles led the British Invasion, and immediately turned his attention toward rock.

Chase's four lead trumpets produced a plangent Valkyrie shriek in four part harmony sufficient to blow down walls. And as a jazz rock outfit, that's what they did. Chase was the loudest band I ever saw. Had to be 125 decibels in that club. During the break my friend Richard said to Bill Chase, "You guys are great but you're too loud!"

"And we're going to get louder!" Chase replied.

Choosing four lead trumpets proved canny in at least one sense—automobile radios are much kinder to upper registers than lowers. There was no hiding from those trumpets, in a club or in a car.

The first album was called *Chase* and featured liner notes by Nat Hentoff. Coming out of Vegas, Chase brought with him some theatrical conventions of which he might not have been aware. *Chase* sounds a little pussy-obsessed and loungey but none of this detracts from their undeniable virtuosity.

"Open Up Wide" begins with a Maynard Ferguson blast and echo effect from Chase as the other trumpets join in one by one like gang members flashing their knives. Furious forward momentum and dazzling upper register trumpet forays, this could be the soundtrack to *Unstoppable* or *Runaway Train*. Each trumpeter whips out his high-wire act—it's an undeniably thrilling and jazz-like performance. But no vocal.

"Livin' In Heat" might have come from 38 Special or some other Southern-fried rocker. Chase holds a piercing trumpet blast like a sustained guitar note for ten seconds.

Terry Richards sings in a robust tenor with grit and a soupçon of dinner theater. Angel South's guitar hisses.

"Hello Groceries" opens with an over-the-top trumpet fanfare. The horns hold back as Richards soulfully croons, "You look so fine, tender and sweet, you're Grade-A inspected meat!"

"Handbags and Gladrags" becomes a gorgeous compendium of falling chords framing Richards' burly vocal.

"Get It On" was Chase's radio hit spending thirteen weeks on the charts in 1971. The trumpets frame Richards' vocal until the bridge when they leap atop one another like trained dolphins creating complex descending figures, a Busby Berkeley horn arrangement. Richards' vocal is pure Vegas.

Jim Peterik, who was later to join Chase, provided "Boys and Girls Together." It features a *sotto voce* section where the horns delicately intertwine before plunging back into the *Sturm und Drang*. Peterik wrote and sang the hit single "Vehicle" for the Ides of March. James William Guercio produced that record, as well as Chicago and BS&T. Thus, Chase is only once removed from the Guercio camp. Frank Rand and Bob Destocki produced all three of the Chase albums.

The fourteen-minute "Invitation to a River" suite holds your attention primarily through virtuoso trumpet performances, beginning with Chase's Iberian blast leading to an attenuated fanfare. "Stay" is the slow section with a repeating bass motif leading to a three-part vocal bridge followed by a series of complex descending trumpet lines that fall away leaving Bill and his echoplex painting profligate arpeggios scampering into the distance like escaping mink.

Their second album *Ennea* (Greek for nine) came out in '72 and shows the band more comfortable with its sound. Chase said in a *Downbeat* interview, "I don't want people to be heavily conscious of a trumpet section. They should just hear good things, but not be clobbered over the head with brass."

New addition G.G. Shinn sings Stephen Foster's "Swanee River" as a Tom Jones flag-waver with dissonant chords contributing to an ominous atmosphere that resolves into a series of rising major arpeggios. You would be hard-pressed to find Foster's original melody in here.

"So Many People" sounds like a BS&T song. The mid-tempo loper features an impassioned G.G. Shinn vocal and gorgeous overlapping trumpets. "Night" begins like a *Twilight Zone* episode but soon switches up into an ominous supernatural thriller with Shinn's banshee vocal matching the trumpets and shredding his larynx.

"It Won't Be Long" begins with a fanfare that Tower of Power might have written. The trumpets sound like the Four Seasons with their doo-wop fashioned charts and Chase taking the Frankie Valli part as Shinn does his best Tom Jones impersonation.

"Woman of the Dark" begins with Chase's clarion. The trumpets answer like a coalescing herd and soon Chase has them in full stampede. This has terrific bones with a great hook of which the trumpets make the most. Shinn's burly voice naturally falls into Tom Jones-like grooves. Following verse-chorus-verse the trumpets take off like acrobatic grackles upping one another with graceful aerial maneuvers. They all join together in a Gordian knot at the end of the instrumental interlude.

The six-part Ennea Suite consists of "Cronus," "Zeus," "Poseidon," "Aphrodite Part I," "Aphrodite Part II," and

"Hades." "Cronus" begins with a theatrical proclamation—Jack Buchanan in *The Band Wagon*—just to let you know that what follows is Classic, a musical *Clash of the Titans*. Somehow, we are not on Mt. Olympus but back in Vegas as the horns sound a fanfare for the entrance of an Ultimate Fighter.

Following Shinn's dire vocal, guitarist Angel South tests the water with a modal raga behind which the horns throw down splashes of color. "Zeus" begins with Phil Porter's moody, Phantom-esque organ leading to Shinn shouting, "ZEUS! ZEUS!" as if calling a dog. Porter traces musical arabesques with his right hand. The song keeps kickin' it up a notch until Shinn is singing in an over-the-top soprano....

"Poseidon" is a fast-paced paean to the sea god with a rising chorus of trumpets that sounds like the orchestral tune-up from "A Day in the Life." Chase delivers a choppy mellifluous solo that ends on a high note. Bill's fragile muted melody leads into "Aphrodite Part I," a ballad. In "Part II" Angel South spaces out a raga with his sitar-sounding guitar. Chase sounds a little like Miles here backed by a muted trumpet section followed by a ratcheting of intensity and Shinn's hefty tremolo.

"Hades" features bass and drums trading fours until Shinn belts the lead with devilish glee. Chase adds an impossible high note as an exclamation mark.

Chase's third album, *Pure Music*, is the least rock-like of the bunch with most of the material straight ahead electric jazz sans vocals. Chase's "Weird Song #1" starts with loping bass and drums, layers on the middle and then the surprisingly subdued trumpets with Chase soloing in a minor mode. This could be a Buddy Rich song. Guitarist John Emma is all elliptical feedback culminating in multiple trumpet fanfares and a segue into "Run Back to Mama," which Chase wrote with Jim Peterik.

Peterik sings "Run Back to Mama" with theatricality reminiscent of The Sweet and the horns have an Ides of March sound to them, at least until they split into some stunning fanfare.

"Twinkles" is another Chase instrumental seducing you with mournful trumpet that explores a lonely wind-swept province.

Bassist Dartanyan Brown sustains the beat until piano, guitar and trumpet tumble gently back in and out leaving Chase to taper into darkness by himself.

"Bochawa" is another Chase instrumental, a mid-tempo marcher, trumpets building a complex pyramid that serves as a launching point for each trumpeter to solo. The new trumpeters included Jim Oatts, Jay Sollenberger and Joe Morrissey. The trumpets follow disparate lines before braiding themselves together in a triumphant weave. Keyboard player Wally Yohn solos like Sunday come to Jesus meeting, the ensemble steps up a notch to the musical equivalent of a cardiac infarction, but beautiful.

Peterik's "Love is on the Way" is probably the best jazz rock song the band did, a barn burner with a killer hook. (www.jimpeterik.com) Curiously, Peterik makes no mention of Chase on his website. He was probably their best singer.

The album ends with Chase instrumental "Close Up Tight," another killer big band big-balled bodacious brassy blast from the Sheik of Shriek. In a valedictorian mood, Chase gives every instrumentalist his due and no one comes up short. It ends with the trumpets repeating the same motif with increasing intensity until Bill comes in and puts his foot down with a resounding blast.

Unfortunately, Bill Chase died at age 39 in 1974 in a plane crash on his way to an appearance in Minnesota. The crash also took the lives of keyboardist Wally Yohn, drummer Walter Clark, and guitarist John Emma.

CHAPTER 15
BITS AND PIECES

Not all the new jazz rock bands were critical or commercial successes. Columbia, home to more horn rock bands than any other label, signed The Flock in 1969. The Flock was a Chicago group with horns and a violinist. They were certainly different. The personnel included Fred Glickstein (guitar, lead vocals), Jerry Goodman (violin), Jerry Smith (bass,) Ron Karpman (drums), Rick Caniff (saxophone), Tom Webb (saxophone) and Frank Rosa (trumpet). (If there's one area in which Wikipedia excels its descriptions of pop culture, it's here.)

Critics praised The Flock for its innovative instrumentation and writing. Saxophonist Tom Webb had been present during the taping of Miles Davis' *Bitches Brew* and brought that sensibility to his compositions. Miles' new direction had precious little to do with melody. The Flock were spacier and less linear than the other bands, but they sound both fussy and incoherent. The songs on the first album are a grab bag of changes that fail to coalesce into a style, or even a hummable tune. The best song is the Kinks' "Tired of Waiting," which begins with Goodman furiously sawing away. Fred Glickstein's vocal can't compare to Ray Davies, but you couldn't kill this song with a bunker bomb.

The last song is "The Truth," a fifteen-minute blues that feels like the Bataan Death March. Mayall, who wrote the liner notes to *The Flock*, does this sort of thing much better.

Dinosaur Swamps came out in '70 and was more successful with all original compositions seemingly inspired by the Museum of Natural History cover art showing pterodactyls flying above a prehistoric canyon. A theme emerges from the jaunty "Green Slice" and is reprised throughout the record. "Big Bird" builds on that momentum in a tuneful jazzy romp dedicated to the pterodactyl. Goodman's violin smears add unique coloration and when trumpeter Frank Posa takes off we take off with him. Jug-band inspired percussion bookends the song.

"Hornschmeyer's Island" begins with ominous rumbling clouds and a delicate chamber music interlude of guitar and violin. The song alternates periods of quiet introspection with a boisterous carnival sound and when the horns start playing arpeggios it all comes together. Goodman's ethereal solo above the rhythm section makes perfect sense.

"Lighthouse" begins with Tom Webb's baritone fog horn. Glickstein is a distinctive singer who tends to arc above the melody. His guitar playing is concise and immediate, but like so much of the Flock's material, the song lacks distinctive bones. There's no hook or chorus on which you can hang your hat. I'll bet these songs were worked out in blowing sessions but unlike Chicago, the band fails to deliver a vision.

"Crabfoot" is a jump blues, one of their stronger compositions with a downhill dynamic, Goodman functioning as part of the horn section, and great vocal call and response between Caniff and Glickstein. The bridge flirts with dissonance leading to bongo madness with horns and violin trading riffs. Karpman drums up the Banzai Pipeline before relaunching with an irresistible funk beat.

"Mermaid" sounds like a Celtic sea chantey with major chords. Horns and violin provide a lush backdrop that suggests the theme music to a romantic comedy.

The Flock released a third album after Goodman had joined the Mahavishnu Orchestra and it fell flat.

Cold Blood was an eight or nine piece, depending, backing bluesy rock belter Lydia Pense whom some compared to Janis Joplin. The three (or four) piece horn section contained some real talent, especially Danny Hill on sax, and guitarist Larry Field was more than capable. However the band failed to make much impact despite four albums. They had no hit singles and a rather generic sound. Their second album was called *Sisyphus*. From the liner notes: "Sisyphus, son of Aeolus, the wind god, a mortal founded Corinth and peopled it with men sprung from mushrooms. He betrayed secrets of the gods and Zeus sent Pluto out to capture Sisyphus." Greeks again! What is it with these jazz rock bands and their Greek gods? All of Cold Blood's output is available on CD.

Satisfaction was the brainchild of Brit trumpeter Mike Cotton who had been fronting bands since the Fifties, including The Mike Cotton Jazzmen, the Mike Cotton Band, and the Mike Cotton Sound. His band backed Solomon Burke, Gene Pitney, the Four Tops, and Stevie Wonder on their English tours. In 1970, Cotton asked guitarist Derek Griffiths to join him in forming Satisfaction. The other players included trombonist John Beecham, Saxophonists Lem Lubin and Nick Newell, and drummer Bernie Higginson. The six piece band achieved a remarkable sound, comparable at times to Chicago and Dreams. Their single eponymous release was recorded in single takes without over tracking.

Satisfaction features a close-up of a garish mouth licking its lips (next to which the Sticky Fingers logo is a model of decorum) and inside the booklet an unappealing photo of a man trying to scratch his own back. Dudes. Fortunately, the recording is much better than the cover art might indicate.

Satisfaction begins with "Just Lay Back and Enjoy It" with layered vocals and tight tight horns. The mid-tempo flag waver tiptoes into a baroque dual flute interlude that pussy-foots to a stop. The guitar enters leading the horn section in a bittersweet chorus that makes good use of dissonance followed by intricate interplay and an ascending chart set against Griffith's fuzz-heavy guitar. They touch magic in this first track and it's a shame the band didn't last.

"She Follows the Band" suggests Traffic in its flute-driven folk chords. Each player has equal say—Satisfaction has a huge sound for six pieces. "Cold Summer" evokes the Sons of Champlin's "Can You Feel It" before Satisfaction veers into its own fast-flowing bluesy river with Traffic and Spencer Davis overtones. Drummer Bernie Higginson is a monster, coloring everything with rolling thunder.

"Sharing" is a modal mostly instrumental that breaks out into a Gil Evans-ish fanfare that launches a probing three-horn foray straight out of Evans' playbook. Bass and drums become insistent until the horns sourly signal the end of the line.

The Chase-like "Call You Liar, Liar" is a no-good girlfriend song with full press rock dynamics and should have been a huge hit for them with a mid-song tempo change that puts guitarist Griffiths front and center with his fleet fuzztone.

"You Upset the Grace of Living When You Lie" has a Fairport Convention/Gentle Giant vibe in its acoustic, flute-comped opening. Obviously the boys had problems with lying girlfriends. Newall channels Sonny Criss on alto. "Just Like Friends" feels like Indigo Girls until the horns slice through.

"Go Through Changes" is their Age of Aquarius song with quasi-philosophical ruminations, but it's the sound that counts. The horn phrasings sound eerily similar to Chicago, particularly when Beecham takes lead on his trombone. No one will mistake him for Pankow, though. The kick-out turns into a blowing jam with Nick Newall honkin' on tenor followed by Cotton who pushes the echoplex. Everyone drops out but bass and guitar who pursue an eerie acoustic blues chord into a wall of massive feedback.

It's all here—good bones, jazz soloing, and a little outside.

CHAPTER 16
LIGHTHOUSE

Lighthouse was a ten- (sometimes thirteen-) piece jazz rock orchestra with a string section and one of the most popular Canadian bands during the early seventies. Drummer Skip Prokop formed the band in the summer of '68 at the urging of jazz vibraphonist Paul Hoffert, who became the second member. Guitarist Ralph Cole rounded out the triumvirate who began auditioning players for a most audacious band.

"'Lighthouse spent nearly two years and three albums in the commercial wilderness trying to figure out what they optimally should sound like. Revamped in the second half of 1970, the group entered a golden period that included three superb studio albums and one career-defining live LP. Dark days began to set in early in 1973, the group, for all intents and purposes, grinding to a halt in August, 1974." (Liner notes to *The Best of Lighthouse* [Universal Music Canada] by Rob Bowman.)

Lighthouse was so huge that they could never fit the whole band into a recording studio at one time. The rock unit would record its part. Days later the string unit recorded followed by the horns. The only recording in which the band was all present was *Lighthouse Live!* (at Carnegie Hall), about which more anon.

Apart from Prokop, Hoffert and Cole the line-up consisted of brass players Freddie Stone, Russ Little and Arnie Chycoski, reed player Howard Shore, string players Ian Guenther, Don Dinovo, Don Whitton, and Leslie Schneider, singer Vic "Pinky" Dauvin and bassist Grant Fullerton. The first album on RCA had serious recording problems and the band sounded muffled. It wasn't until they moved to record label GRT that their studio albums did them any justice.

Is Lighthouse jazz rock? It's a problematic question. The tightly arranged studio recordings left little room to move and most of the songs, co-written by Prokop and other band members, fell into a hortatory Age of Aquarius bag, much like their counterpoints to the south, the Sons of Champlin. On the other hand Prokop and company knew how to write a solid hit with at least three chords and soaring choruses. The exquisite over-the-top falsetto harmony is a hallmark of their many songs.

Best of Lighthouse begins with "Sunny Days," a brash big band ode to "lying in the sun listening to rock and roll." Beginning with a bluesy piano vamp the horns come in like any big band of the forties. The chorus with its show-biz melody hooks you instantly. This sounds like the theme song to some nostalgia-drenched romantic comedy set at summer camp.

The exhilarating "You Girl" begins with violas chugging away with art house tension. Enter the contrapuntal guitar that switches from acoustic to electric and the song takes an unexpected turn toward Laura Nyro with its gorgeous chorus. Stacked vocal harmonies top out around 30,000 feet.

"Take It Slow," another anthem for Hippy Nation, might have come off an early Sons of Champlin session except for that signature falsetto harmony. This is Lighthouse. "House in the Country," "Island of Love," and "In the Country." Lighthouse's exuberant response to the Age of Aquarius is the musical equivalent of Rand Holmes' comics. Rand Holmes was a Canadian artist whose exquisite, Wally Wood-derived style, preached a peace and love gospel. Holmes ultimately practiced what he preached, moving to a remote island off British

Columbia where he spent the rest of his life creating comics, of which *Harold Hedd* is the most famous.

Check out *Rand Holmes: The Artist Himself* by Patrick Rosenkranz (Fantagraphics).

In their coveralls, work shirts and hats, Lighthouse looks like a farming commune. Looking at this ancient cover art it's amazing how many of these big city kids strived to look like farmers or tradesmen. Bloomfield, running from his multi-million-dollar inheritance. Seatrain: coveralls, shirtless, posing on a hillside in the sun. The notorious Byrd Brothers decked out like desperadoes. Chicago, posing with antique revolvers and buffalo guns in furs.

Dramatic piano introduces the lilting "Good Day," another love letter to life with a great Jim Messina-like melody and a monster hook. There are horns and strings in here but it's not jazz rock, it's just great orchestral pop.

"1849" comes closest to defining Lighthouse, melding their huge sound with a worthy topic, the Gold Rush. This ironic history lesson packs a surprising emotional punch in its overview of a wagon train heading west. A golden age theater fanfare leads into a chorus singing "They headed west in 1849, 61 wagons two-miles long in a line...." The bridge is to die for, the chorus heavenly.

"Pretty Lady" begins with a Tower of Power quality fanfare. No jazz, but it's a great song as are most on this Best Of compilation.

Lighthouse Live! was recorded at Carnegie Hall in 1972 and for a two mike pick-up the sound quality is exceptional. According to Hoffert this is the record that best exemplifies the group. Songs that seem somewhat generic on record take on stronger personalities live. This is particularly true of the opener, "I Just Wanna Be Your Friend," which takes on a rocking Bonnie and Delaney vibe. "Take It Slow" gathers huge momentum like a human wave that builds to the achingly beautiful bridge. "Old Man's" fast-moving horn section sounds like a much bigger band. Hoffert's vibes give Lighthouse a unique quality. The song

A Brief History of Jazz Rock

slows for an elegiac violin solo, the cellos chime in and then everyone drops out leaving Larry Smith's bluesy *a capella* trombone to bring the song to a soft landing.

"Rockin Chair" is a fast blues, something Edgar Winter might play. "You and Me" has an all-strings soap opera intro that morphs into real opera with an aria that Bizet might have written. Keith Jollimore takes lead on flute putting in plenty of phlegm before handing off to Cole's stadium guitar. "Sweet Lullaby" is a fat, leisurely ballad with all the trimmings. "1849" creeps up on you like a ninja army and suddenly the song is tugging at your heart, like something out of *Les Mis*.

Finally there is the much-ballyhooed eighteen minute version of "Eight Miles High." Following a long guitar intro the voices enter stacked eight miles high with Keith Jollimore's baritone honking down below like an alien phaser. The arrangement gives everyone plenty of room to make a statement, cello by cello, horn by horn and while there's some excellent use of space here the whole thing doesn't hang together convincingly and none of the soloists lift you out of your seat.

Lighthouse may not have been jazz rock, but they were a big band with a big heart and big songs and are worth a listen. They were the Polyphonic Spree of their day.

CHAPTER 17
MALO

Most people have heard of Carlos Santana, the Bay Area rocker who has been tearing up arenas for over thirty years. Santana's big hit "Oye Como Va" was written by the late, great Latin jazz leader Tito Puente. Santana's version gave new life to Tito's later career. I saw Tito Puente and his band in Madison, WI in 1994 and they kicked ass.

Less people know about Carlo's younger brother Jorge and his band Malo. Jorge's first band was the Malibus, a nine piece R&B outfit with horns (no relation to the current LA band of that name). In 1971, they changed their name to Malo and signed with Warner Brothers. Initial members included singer Arcelio Garcia, Jr., Jorge on guitar, Abel Zarate on lead guitar and vocals, bassist Pablo Tellez, drummer Richard Spremich, pianist Richard Kermode, and trumpeters Luis Gasca and Roy Murray. Guest musicians included Coke Escovedo on timbales, Victor Pantoja on congas and bones, and Richard Bean who sings the lead on "Suavecito," their biggest hit.

The Malibus had been playing "Suavecito" for years but it didn't become a hit until the release of the first Malo album, *Malo*. With its furious, multi-layered rhythms, exquisite ensemble sound and brilliant soloing, Malo was the jazziest of jazz rock outfits. Granted this is *heavily* in the Latin jazz tradition, but the Latin jazz contribution is just as important as the blues.

Malo's cover art is a stunning painting by Jesus Helguera whose work compares favorably with that of N.C. Wyeth, Howard Pyle and Maxfield Parrish. Helguera painted heroic, larger-than-life Latino gods and goddesses. He was a Mexican Alex Ross.

"Pana" bursts from the gates in hammered silver and brass splendor. This is what Dizzy would play were he alive today. The similarity to Afro-Cuban music was there from the git go. The band has an enormous sound due primarily to Richard Kermode's out-front piano and that crazy rhythm section laying down a chop that could raise Franco. Although the emphasis is on brass Murray also plays sax and flute, reducing the shrill factor. Garcia and Zarate chant the vocals to the break where the rhythm doubles up beneath a pitch perfect Gasca trumpet solo. The horns drop out to leave the rhythm section choogling like a well-oiled machine until Kermode picks up the simple theme on piano to bring it home.

"Just Say Goodbye" starts as a pensive ballad delineated by Jorge on guitar but takes an abrupt up-tempo swerve that builds tension with Kermode's organ swell until Jorge leaps out front with a visceral solo that makes much out of few notes. The tonic shifts up a tone, down a tone and slows way down. The voices enter as a wordless chorus that disappears into a tunnel ceding to an aquatic bass and Garcia's mournful vocal accompanied by Jorge's keening guitar. At nearly eight minutes it doesn't feel padded at all. All six songs on the first record are long with the longest, "Peace," clocking in at 9:21. They simply didn't have that much material.

"Cafe's" magnetic rhythms grab you by your belt buckle and pull you into a simmering Latin beat. Garcia sings in Spanish but it doesn't matter—the rhythms and melody are seductive on their own. Jorge speaks the universal language of blistering guitar—his playing reminds me a little of Zappa's in his use of modality and avoiding the usual tension/release format. Jorge shares lead guitar duties with Abel Zarate and when they "weave" they sound like a Latin Rolling Stones. Dig that crazy dual line on the outro.

"Nena's" galloping rhythm section leads into a classic horn riff. This one sounds like their later hit, "Latin Bugaloo" with sharp little flute accents over the horn section. Garcia sings, "Baby, I want to dance with you." A horn fanfare launches Murray on trombone followed by Gasca on trumpet. Kermode's piano solo has a Zen-like simplicity. He shades it in more on organ. If any band can get away with less than three chords it's Malo, whose rhythm section is endlessly fascinating, like staring into a fireplace.

"Suavecito" begins as languid ballad with Richard Bean singing the pastoral theme. Ironically it's one of their less interesting tunes, mainly carried on the back of the rhythm section.

"Peace" is their Summer of Love song and begins in a bluesy groove but shifts into an almost Celtic melody with Murray's soprano. The song tapers to silence from which Gasca's trumpet rises like a mourning dove, but soon kicks it up into a post-bop groove, something the Jazz Messengers might have played. Everyone drops out but bass and guitar, who turn up the heat to a hard rock fever. The horns jump back in to the blues groove intensely.

I used to have *Dos* on vinyl. It had a beautiful jacket with the Malo symbol embossed on plain cardboard. The CD is only available as an import, for more than a hundred dollars. Fortunately, three of the five songs are available on *The Best of Malo*. They include: "Oye Mama," "I'm For Real," and "Latin Bugaloo," and they comprise the best of early Malo.

"Oye Mama" begins with a thrilling trumpet fanfare that might herald the entrance of the primo matador. The rhythm section erupts with irrepressible *joie de vivre* as Garcia sings the Spanish lyrics propelled by sharp trumpet blasts. The horns carry the melody into a starburst of exploding brass, the audio equivalent of fireworks at Disney World. Pianist Kermode channels Chucho Valdes with his highly rhythmic and forceful touch—somewhere between Dave Brubeck and Cecil Taylor. Congas, timbales and drums trade feverish fours. The rhythm section sucks you in like a whirlpool, works you over like ten Swedish masseurs and when it stops you wipe the drool off your mouth, look up and say, "Is that all?"

"I'm For Real" lulls you with pastoral synthesized strings and flute, enter Garcia singing in English up to the bridge where the rhythm doubles down and ballad morphs to power ballad. Coke Escovedo's timbales are all over this like spots on a leopard. Roy Murray carries it out on soprano sax.

"Latin Bugaloo" is a runaway train. Fiery horns cede to pinprick slam-dunk piano underwriting Garcia's English vocal. At 2:41 it flashes by with a whoosh leaving you wondering. Where did it go?

Evolution was Malo's third album and their last for Warner Brothers. It contains "Dance to My Mambo," another runaway train with an unforgettable horn line. The mambo is Cuban but that horn line is pure mariachi. Piano and horns trade fast lines over the bouncin' rhythm. You'd have to be dead to sit still through this. Gasca's trumpet arcs like a sun flare over a rhythm as vast and choppy as the Caribbean during hurricane season.

CHAPTER 18
THE HOOK

Music writers are always referring to a song's hook, that sweet release that comes after the tension of the bridge. Tension and release is the foundation of all art, particularly the performing arts. There is much misunderstanding of what actually constitutes a hook.

From Wikipedia: *A hook is a musical idea, a passage or phrase, that is believed to be appealing and make the song stand out. Hooks are "meant to catch the ear of the listener" (Covach 2005, p.71). Hooks generally apply to popular music, especially rock music and pop music subgenres such as dance music.*

A hook can, in general, be either melodic or rhythmic, and often incorporates the main motif for a piece of music. Characteristics of a melodic hook include skips in the tonal line; however, details of what makes a tune "catchy" are difficult to describe. A rhythmic hook can be equally catchy by employing syncopation or other devices, but there are still examples of rhythmic hooks which are very straightforward.

Hooks are often used in music research by radio stations and record companies to gauge the popularity of various songs.

In song, hooks usually come at the end of the chorus, or lead into it, making the lyrics come to the height or "point" of the song.

John Davis, a founding member of the White Trash Blues Band and the academic journal *The Velvet Light Trap*, says, "In general, I would say all forms of commercial entertainment need a hook to grab the audience, something that makes that particular book, movie, or song stand out from the rest. At the same time, the most common hooks are sex and violence. Would Beyoncé, or Lady Gaga be so popular if they weren't so good looking? Would rappers like 50 Cent be so popular without the level violence in their songs?

"Musically, a hook can be many things, a lyric, a horn riff, a key change, a solo, a beat, etc. You would need to look at each particular song (or music video) and ask yourself what is the particular hook of that song."

Bill Champlin says, "It's usually the chorus of the song which repeats regularly. Sometimes it's a handclap in the right place, but that's more of an A&R or DJ definition."

Phil Davis (no relation to John), co-founder of Firetown, describes a hook as, "A song lyric, rhythm riff or melodic line, usually, repetitive, that 'hooks' the listener."

Bruce Brodeen, chief cook and bottle washer for Not Lame Records and Rockandrolltribe, says, "The sticky, subconscious part of a song's DNA that attaches itself to the brain's memory stem and will not let go until it is acknowledged and enjoyed by the music lover at a manifest, conscious level."

Ben Sidran (www.bensidran.com), a Bonnaroo jazz pianist who wrote "Space Cowboy" for the Steve Miller Band (of which he was a member) says, "A hook is the payoff, the point, the spear to the heart, the worm in the ear, the woman in the back booth, something so simple you can whistle along with it before it ends, the rubber meeting the road, the reason for the whole affair ... otherwise, it ain't a hook."

Mark the airline pilot says, "The song 'Killing Floor' by Albert King (which appears on The Electric Flag: *A Long Time Comin'*) is a 12-bar Blues. It has a great ascending guitar riff that plays in the first measure, and then repeats in every measure of the song. That ascending riff (doubled by the bass) is the hook for that song. It repeats itself over and over, and "is" the song. I can't remember many of the words, but I can play that hook in my sleep.

"The Blues Standard 'Kansas City' has a very recognizable hook, the melody. Sing to yourself:

1 1 1 1

I'm Going to Kansas City, Kansas City here I come, (melodic response, usually guitar)

4 4 1 1

I'm going to Kansas City, Kansas City here I come, (another response, usually unchanged)

5 4 1 1

they got crazy little women, god I'm gonna get me one (turnaround)

"The melodic line 'I'm going to Kansas City' is the songs main hook. It repeats itself through the call and the response. Everyone recognizes it. It more or less dominates the first eight bars and in this song is the most recognizable feature, therefore the hook. On the 5 is a line that is rhythmically the same but melodically different in this song. It goes 'they got crazy little women' over the 5 chord. and 'God I'm gonna' over the 4 chord, which is melodically similar to the line over the 5, and then finishes with two measures of the one chord. the 5 chord is just a recognizable part of the blues standard that signals that you are starting the last 4 bar movement of the song, and getting ready to repeat the 12 bars over again ... and again ... and again. It has no significant correlation with a hook. The hook could be placed over the 5 chord, probably a horn based riff (or hook if you will).

"When you think of a 'guitar or instrumental hook,' look at the intro riff to 'Mary had a Little Lamb.' SRV's Guitar riff at the beginning of the song, first half pre-measure, or count-in is his 'Signature Hook.'"

Fair enough, but not far enough. For me, you can't have a hook unless a song has at least three chords. One and two chord songs just don't cut it. The hook is caused by a series of chords that demand resolution—they create a tipping point, an untenable sound that can only be resolved by a chord that feels right to the ear. Wiki is right that the hook usually comes at the end of the chorus but not always. Let's look at a couple Beach Boys songs for their hook.

"I Get Around" is pretty straightforward and states the hook right out of the gate. But it doesn't become the hook until after the soaring chorus. First we hear the chorus beginning with "Round round get around I get around," then the song breaks into the tonic. "I'm getting' bugged driving up and down the same old strip/I gotta find a new place where the kids are hip." Second chorus. Then comes a repeat of the chorus but this time with a bridge that nudges the song up a chord: "I'm a real cool head, I'm making real good bread." There follows a traditional Beach Boys doo-wop leading back to the chorus, "Round round get around I get around."

"Good Vibrations," which writer Brian Wilson called a "pocket symphony," begins with a heavenly chorus that almost sighs, "I love the colorful clothes she wears, and the way the sunlight plays upon her hair...." There's two chords right there plus the next verse. The hook is, "I'm pickin' up good vibrations/She's giving me excitations...." See how it neatly resolves the tension created by the ethereal yearning of the first two chords? That's a hook!

After reading the above three paragraphs Mark the airline pilot said, "There are two rigidly flexible rules in music.

"1. To create tension do one of the following: create a phrase or pitch movement that is ascending in pitch (scale, arpeggio, glissando on a piano, violin or pennywhistle). A descending pitch movement results in resolution. Increase volume or intensity and you get tension. Reduce volume or intensity and you get resolution (fff to ppp). Play a pitch that is dissonant over a chord movement and you get tension. Resolve that to a consonant pitch and you get resolution. 'Maria, I just met a girl named Maria' goes from major to a dissonant tritone, then resolves.

"2. Once a rule is thoroughly understood, it can be thoroughly broken! This is original. Think of tension as an event that breaks normality. You are eating corn on the cob. Normal, enjoyable summertime thing. Suddenly you get a big kernel of corn stuck between your teeth. Dissonant, tension-building event. Normalcy is broken and you want it back. Get a piece of floss and remove the kernel. Release! You feel great. The release of tension may even make you feel better than you did a few minutes earlier before the errant piece of corn added dissonance to your moment!!

"Musicians think in phrases. Songwriters think in 'hooks.' A trumpet player being coached prior to an important audition may be told to watch his phrasing, not his 'hooks.' Songwriters like Burt Bacharach write phrases which are intended to get our attention. It is assumed that when Burt writes a phrase, or song, he automatically puts tension and release into the phrase.

"Rests in music are another example. When coaching my sons on their instruments, I have them slowly play the phrase, then exhale during the rests to make sure that the emptiness is recognized and emphasized. Take a 4/4 measure: one-and-two-and-three-and-four.

"Put rests on the upbeats, (the 'ands') and you have a resolving march. You feel good like Souza! Life make perfect sense. Put the rest on the down beat (one-AND-two-AND-three-AND-four) and just play the 'ands' and you have funk.

"Tension and resolution are very subjective, Your argument is that a sensation is a hook is interesting."

So I hope that clears things up.

CHAPTER 19
BACK TO CHICAGO

By '72 jazz rock fervor had abated. Although Chicago and BS&T would continue for decades, their grip on the popular imagination had slipped in the face of new detonations in popular music. The seventies saw Stevie Wonder's incredible four album run, starting with *Music of My Mind*. This, along with *Talking Book*, *Innervisions*, and *Fulfillingness' First Finale* constitute the greatest series of knock-out pop albums since the Beatles.

The seventies saw the rise of soul music's three great mutations: Earth, Wind and Fire, Graham Central Station, and Parliament-Funkadelic. EWF and Parliament are still active today. Although there is little improv on their records, these groups used horns and drew on jazz traditions.

The seventies saw the emergence of Talking Heads and Bruce Springsteen. It saw the explosion in fusion music initiated by Miles Davis on *Bitches Brew*. John McLaughlin's Mahavishnu Orchestra (including violinist Jerry Goodman from the Flock), Chick Corea's Return to Forever and Larry Coryell's The Eleventh House emerged as major fusion players. Lenny White, Billy Cobham, Hal Galper. All led fusion. Fusion bands are not jazz rock. They represent a new direction in jazz with a fleeter, more electric bass and more emphasis on electronics.

Butterfield dead, Bloomfield dead, Dreams dissipated, it was left to Chicago and Blood, Sweat and Tears to carry on, to carry on. Chicago's first two records established new standards in jazz rock and pop music never to be equaled. Never again would the band have the luxury to work out their arrangements for weeks or months at their leisure. Now they had to produce, bing, bang, bam. However, later Chicago records are not without interest. *Chicago V* was a milestone: their first single disc! It also yielded "Saturday in the Park," a great song by any measure. By now everybody knows that Robert Lamm wrote the song after walking through Central Park on the 4th of July.

"Saturday in the park, I think it was the 4th of July." The best art is artless.

Let's back up. *V* starts with "A Hit by Varese," an urgent, angular vehicle with the horns smearing all over the place like motorists careening out of control on an icy road. The horn section solos one by one and end up trading fours like a trio of craps shooters eager for the next roll. The nearly five minute song is radio antagonistic—at least in terms of what was commercial back then—but Chicago more than make up for it with "All is Well," a swooning ballad that makes excellent use of the three singers. Lamm's vocal is quintessentially Midwestern in vowels and attitude followed by a thrusting, harmonious horn passage that dabbles in dissonance.

"Now That You've Gone," with its constantly shifting vocals highlights the horn section's "Chicago Chord."

"Dialogue (Parts One and Two)" is another slab of Robert Lamm genius, two dudes discussing the state of the world. One (Kath) is concerned, one (Peter) not so much. "Don't you ever worry when you see what's going down?" "No, I try to mind my business, that is, no business at all." Love that "going down." "Don't it make you angry the way war is dragging on? Well, I hope the President knows what he's into, I don't know." The more things change ... The song marches into the chorus "We can change the world now ... we can save the children...." Kath launches a fat wobbler with his wah-wah pedal. And the song fades out on three-part *a capella*. Would such a hopeful, naive, song stand a chance in today's cynical, balkanized, angry market?

CAN YOU HEAR US, LADY GAGA?!

"While the City Sleeps" derives much of its urgency from Cetera's pumping bass. Minor stuff.

Everything about "Saturday in the Park" is iconic, from Lamm's sprightly piano intro to Cetera's booming bass to the horns' joyful blips. Can you dig it? Yes I can. The song opens up on the rocking, syncopated "Slow Motion Rider," making it feel bigger than it actually is, like four seasons in one day. Like all their best material "Saturday" has a timeless quality, insuring that it will be around forever.

"State of the Union" starts as standard hard rock but the bridge where Cetera sings, "Then I saw her down in the darkness" lifts the song out of the ordinary. "Goodbye's" graceful fanfare segues into a compelling minor key vocal by Cetera, whose kinetic bass drives the song. Listen to Seraphine's knotty, harmonic drumming. The second movement showcases Pankow's fluid trombone against a typically intriguing horn arrangement.

Chicago V is a very good record.

Blood, Sweat and Tears soldiered on with Clayton-Thomas fronting for two more albums, *3* and *4*. Like Chicago they had given up on actually titling the albums. These two albums—*meh*. Others may differ but I always found them stop-gap and inconsistent, *pace* "Lucretia MacEvil." Of greater interest is *New Blood*, which came out in '72.

The new line-up included singer Jerry Fisher, trombone player Dave Bargeron, reed player Lou Marini, Jr., trumpeters Lew Soloff and Chuck Winfield and guitarist George Wadenius. Original members included guitarist Katz, drummer Colomby and bassist Jim Fielder. Colomby had taken over production duties from Guercio, which may have resulted in this jazzier sound.

Fisher is a smoother singer than Clayton-Thomas and sounds right from the start, Dylan's "Down in the Flood." Katz' harmonica gives it a deep south roadhouse sound. Marini's *a capella* horns are aptly ironic. "Touch Me" strikes me as the wrong kind of song for the band—a sincere ballad. Yeah, good job but so what? This could be any singer in any studio in the world. By the time the horns enter it's a tribute to our fighting forces.

"Alone" is immediately more arresting with its opening horn blast and its promise of future fury. This is the type of sleek horn vehicle at which BS&T excels. An over-the-top escalating riff gives way to a Georg Wadenius' guitar solo in which he evokes sitar. Technically Katz wasn't up to other contemporary guitarists. He's always sounded fine to me, but what Wadenius does here is beyond Katz. Bargeron plays a great tuba solo and the ensemble rolls tightly back in.

"Velvet" is a stunning bittersweet ballad about a horse written by Dreams' Jeff Kent. Any song about an animal—I go to pieces. And this is a good one, all golden harmonies and restraint. "I Can't Move No Mountains" is more like it, a minor-keyed mini-masterpiece with exquisite chords and a heavenly rainbow-colored bridge. Marini's horn arrangement makes good use of dissonance but always pays off with sweet resolution.

Bargeron's "Over the Hill" has a knotty country melody that marches adeptly through a series of clever chord changes like a pack of Sherpas. Good song for Festivus—the first two thirds are complaints about getting old and the final third offers absolution, young and old together. "So Long Dixie" is an elegiac fanfare perfect for the graduation address at Ole Miss.

The last two tracks stand together and above all that has gone before, providing that spark of excitement that kicks the whole band up to another level and makes you think yeah, this is jazz rock. Bergeron and Fielder's arrangement of Goffin/King's "Snow Queen" mines deep that furrow of excitement briefly touched in "I Can't Move No Mountains." The horns define the shape and texture with an irresistible minor key theme that gives way to a bridge so sweet it's like falling into a hot bath. Fisher's trick-free vocal is very effective. Willis, Marini and Bargeron contribute concise cutting solos and man when you hear a trombone solo you know you are in jazz rock land. The horns collapse tightly and Colomby contributes a visceral solo that leads into Herbie Hancock's "Maiden Voyage" and Wadenius' guitar/vocal solo. Jazz rock heaven.

New Blood is a successful transfusion.

CHAPTER 20
TOP POWERS ON

While other bands came and went Tower of Power stuck to it under the steady guidance of Emilio Castillo and Doc Kupka. As leader and main songwriter Castillo was content to lay back and play second alto, ceding star roles to tenor player Lennie Pickett and baritone player Kupka. Kupka's booming baritone was essential to TOP's sound and sets it off from other horn sections.

In 1972, Tower of Power signed with Warner Brothers and released the album *Bump City* with the song, "You're Still a Young Man." Their second WB album, *Tower of Power*, proved to be their most successful and spawned the hit "So Very Hard to Go." While most people who know TOP, if they know them at all, know them for those two songs and "What Is Hip?" TOP's work is far more diversified. They've released twenty-three albums so far. Let's focus on two WB albums that haven't garnered that much attention, *In the Slot* ('75) and *Ain't Nothin' Stoppin' Us Now* ('76).

While the most popular TOP material hews to a modern soul template, they are equally adept at creating up tempo jazz mini-suites tying several cuts together with clever segues and dazzling fanfares. *In the Slot* begins with "Just Enough and Too Much," a flag wavin', booty-shakin' paean to beauty with a nifty stop and go rhythm. Lead singer Hubert Tubbs is typical of the band's singers—great pipes, superb phrasing, a first-rate soul shouter. The sound quality is light years beyond their Fillmore debut.

"Treat Me Like Your Man" is a blue ballad written by three sax players—strong melody, horns arcin' like sun flares. Kupka's baritone is integral to "If I Play My Cards Right," like an elbow in the ribs.

"Fanfare: Matanuska" is a *sui generis* TOP slice of pop funk beginning with what sounds like a violin section but is actually Chester Thompson's synthesizer segueing into syncopation so severe it could snap your neck. Kupka's baritone gooses the song into "On the Serious Side," a rare one-chord foray that pops like the 4th of July. Beat. David Garibaldi's strut leads into "Ebony Jam," a blowing vehicle for Lenny Pickett's smooth Newk-influenced tenor followed by Mic Gillette on trumpet, Bruce Conte on guitar and Chester Thompson who grabs you by the scruff of the neck with his fat organ riff.

"You're So Wonderful, So Marvelous" builds on the previous song's momentum in this joyous soul monster. "Vuela Por Noche" seems like an extension of "Ebony Jam" with its tricky stop and go meter and blowing space, and then the magical Chester Thompson piano intro to the swooning "Essence of Innocence" whose coloration and subject matter recalls the Thad Jones/Mel Lewis Band. Except, of course, TOP is funkier.

The album ends with the funky, irresistible "Drop It In the Slot."

Ain't Nothin Stoppin' Us Now is among their best. It starts with the crack of a cue ball leading into the Graham Central Station-ish title track with Kupka's baritone honkin' the horn section and Edward McGee pumping the vocals. Funk cedes to smooth soul balladry on "By Your Side," Chester Thompson's synthesizer running chills up and down your spine. McGee has sufficient power in his voice that he doesn't have to shout. His eerie, piercing falsetto cuts through the orchestra like a laser.

"Make Someone Happy" is one of those great sunny day songs like "Saturday in the Park," "Groovin'," or "Take It Slow" but with soul. Actually the Rascals had soul. Mic Gillette takes a trumpet break on the bridge that's like a plunge into a cool mountain stream. And listen to Francis Prestia's rolling bass.

"You Ought To Be Havin' Fun" is one of the great party songs beginning with a guitar tingle that tumbles down baritone steps to the chorus, "You ought to be havin' fun...." McGee effortlessly kicks it into the stratosphere and dig that crazy bridge with *a capella* voices chanting, "You ought to be, you ought to be" over the tom-tom beat. Like all great soul it has an indefinable emotional gravity that causes it to linger in the memory long after it's played.

"Can't Stand to See the Slaughter" is a funky condemnation of hypocrisy. "I can't stand air pollution but still I drive a car/Maybe that's the reason why things is like they are." I'd reprint all the lyrics if I could get permission. Maybe we will. Stands pretty good just as a poem. I could get up at a poetry jam and read this and get a standing O. They sing it over fluttering bass and a quasi-military beat with Kupka's baritone booting it in the ass. "Can't Stand" segues flawlessly into the gorgeous big band fanfare of "It's So Nice." McGee sings a difficult falsetto melody flawlessly with a heavenly backing chorus. This could be the theme at Heaven's gate.

"Deal With It" plunges from heavenly bliss to hard-nosed reality in this tough honkin' relationship vehicle that would have been perfect for Marvin Gaye and Tammy Terrell. Kupka's baritone burbles like the La Brea Tar Pits. The song ends abruptly with a startling arching blast of the horns leading straight into their greatest fanfare, the beginning of "While We Went to the Moon," a bittersweet search for ecological balance with a redemptive chorus. McGee imbues his vocal with heartfelt emotion. After the fade-out, the pool ball cracks again and the boys reprise the vocal from "Ain't Nothin'" until the fade away. Some records are like a movie. This is one of them.

CHAPTER 21
PERMUTATIONS

When If broke up in '72, sax player Dave Quincy and guitarist Terry Smith ended up doing a lunchtime gig in a North London pub. One day Loughty Lasisi Amao, sax player for the late, great Osibisa, showed up at the pub. "He was sitting outside waiting for me dressed in his black and white African robes, wearing a bowler hat with his conga drum," Quincy recalls. "He told me he had tracked me down with the idea of forming a new band. Terry and me liked the idea."

The first incarnation of Zzebra included pianist Gus Yeadon, drummer Liam Genockey, and bassist John McCoy. Due to Loughty's involvement *Zzebra* has more of a world-music feel than *If*, with more Afro-centric rhythm jams but it's still first-rate jazz rock. "Cobra Woman" off the eponymous first album is a slinky slice of swamp rock lit by Smith's incendiary guitar. Gus Yeadon is an appropriately sinister and evocative lead singer. Loughty takes a lighter touch with his baritone than Kupka might, but you know it's there especially on the bridge. The versatile Loughty switches to flute for the second movement, which slides through logical and pleasing changes. More than a soupçon of Santana in this mix.

Loughty's one chord "Mr. J." bubbles up from a simmering rhythm section overlaid with African patois. The rhythmic potboiler is saved from monotony by a surprising vocal chorus and energetic sax work.

The Quincy/Smith/McCoy "Mah Yong" could have come off a Horace Silver record with its blues-based bop feel. Smith solos over nothing but drums and commands our attention with dazzling pointillist runs interspersed with strong blues riffs. Quincy's alto solo writhes almost visibly drawing on Blue Note traditions with a touch of Trane. The Quincy/Amao "Ife" starts as a chant, morphs through some jungle drums, settles into the theme song to a nature documentary. (Imagine a plummy English voice, "Here, in the Valley of Gwangi, the shepherds tend their flocks much as their forefathers have done since time immemorial....")

"Spanish Fly" begins with booming bass and trilling flute before settling into a hard bop one chord groove, Quincy channeling Sonny Fortune on soprano. A couple minutes in the tonic drops a tone launching Smith on a ruminative solo that abruptly stretches its modal wings. When Quincy reenters on soprano these guys sound uncannily like the first edition of Chick Corea's Return to Forever. "Amuso Fi" features Yeadon on vocals over a blues-based riff. Zzebra is more rhythmically interesting than a lot of jazz rock bands due to the interplay between drummers Genockey and Loughty. But they're not as melodically daring as Chicago or Dreams and some of the material verges on potboiler—"Rhythm section vamps and everybody takes a turn."

"Rainbow Train" is one of their more interesting comps with a celebratory theme, ska-touched horns and Yeadon's gritty vocal. The train slows down to negotiate Yeadon's tricky piano curves followed by a guitar tender, then picks up steam on the downhill side. A worthy addition to the long and honorable tradition of train songs that includes Duke Ellington's "Daybreak Express," Wynton Marsalis' "Big Train," Johnny Mercer's "The Atchison, Topeka and the Santa Fe," The Yardbirds' "Train Kept

A-Rollin,'" and Ervin Rouse's "Orange Blossom Special." To name a few.

"Hungry Horse" ends the first album in daring fashion with perfectly matched horns and guitar leaping hurdles with an ascending chorus that erupts into a wobbly Smith guitar solo. Band drops out leaving Smith soloing high-wire, segueing into a series of drum exchanges interspersed with Quincy's soaring soprano. There's a funny vocal near the end.

Zzebra's second album, *Panic*, saw some personnel changes: Steve Byrd replaced Smith on guitar. Alan Marshall became lead singer, Tommy Eyre replaced Yeadon on keys and also played flute. The title tune begins with tight horns. Marshall's urgent singing recalls Lambert, Hendricks and Ross. "You've Lost That Lovin' Feelin'" starts with Quincy limning the familiar theme on soprano to languid syncopation. One waits in vain for the vocal as each member steps forth for a signature statement. Come on, guys! You've got singers! What's the problem? Instead we get a very nice jazz version of a very nice song.

Quincy's "Karrola" exudes a fast fusion vibe. At this point Zzebra sounds like they want to be a fusion band more than they want to appeal to pop fans. When jazz musicians start playing for themselves you can kiss any pop element goodbye. "Liamo" is a mid-tempo vehicle for flute and sax. There's a chanted vocal as part of the ensemble but no lyrics *per se*.

Tommy Eyre's "Death by Drowning" begins with ethereal piano and a smattering of conga. More noodling. Synthesizer whale calls. Enter Quincy in a contemplative mood. Eyre posits the mournful theme on keyboards as Alan Marshall sings the solid lyrics with a baroque change-up in the bridge. The tempo doubles as Eyre solos. He is an intriguing one-handed piano player with traces of Corea and Hal Galper, and he should have contributed more compositions to this record.

The funky "Put a Light On Me" proudly displays its blues roots and layered vocals. Finally, "La Si Si-Lu So So" plunges into a fusion groove with tight ensemble playing, in-your-face drumming, and solo space all around. These cats can blow. But

A Brief History of Jazz Rock

at this stage they are walking away from jazz rock, with its popular appeal, straight into the extremely crowded fusion field. Zzebra put out one last album in *Lost World*, but by then the handwriting was on the wall.

Following the break-up of Colosseum, drummer Jon Hiseman formed the short-lived Tempest. In 1976, Hiseman disbanded Tempest in 1974 and in 1976 formed Colosseum II with guitarist Gary Moore, vocalist Mike Starrs, bassist Neil Murray, and keyboard player Don Airey. Their first release was *Strange New Flesh*. Once you lose the horns the band is more than halfway to fusion but they have a singer and so are included here.

Strange New Flesh has a cool Dali-esque cover depicting the band members as dada constructions. "Dark Side of the Moog" has two sections—a fast and furious first section in which Gary Moore out fusion-kasts Mahavishnu as he and Airey engage in an intense dialogue. Stop-and-go rhythm and intense ensemble work recall King Crimson. Airey airs it out on Moog in a series of arpeggios like cast fishing nets. The second section is built around a repeated minor motif and has a much heavier bottom. It's a compelling duet propelled by Hiseman's bubbling drums but it sounds like a lot of fusion these days.

Guitarist Moore introduces Joni Mitchell's "Down to You" with a romantic statement of the theme with a weird whistling keyboard in the background. Singer Mike Starrs gives it the full ballroom blitz in the slow opening segment with a touch of Freddie Mercury. The song descends into a trickling piano stream in which Don Airey introduces a phrase of lilting beauty that opens up into suite-like proportions. Airey switches to electric, kicks it up a notch and we're in the HVO lane, drummer Hiseman adding density and propulsion until he spits out Moore who repeats that lilting figure. One of the more interesting Joni Mitchell covers.

"Gemini and Leo" is a sleek black low-rider of a song with War-like percussion and Mike Starrs' Robert Plant-like vocal. The syncopated stop-and-go could give you whiplash. "Secret Places" has a Motown vibe that quickly morphs into acid jazz with Airey playing ostinatos behind a heavy metal thrust. Starrs and Moore form a formidable vocal wave between them. "On Second Thoughts" is an instrumental. It's quite expert but nothing you can hum. Finally, "Winds" features Hiseman's strutting drum solo that Billy Cobham would have liked.

This is a very good record but not really in the jazz rock camp. When you think of all the fusion bands who have released records in the past thirty years, your mind melts. There must be three centuries of continuous music on record by now, and that's just for the standard quartets! It must be hellishly difficult for a fusion band to distinguish themselves among the mob these days. I subscribe to *Downbeat* and every issue is chock full of new fusion bands.

CHAPTER 22
HOW TO CLAP

It would behoove us all to get out and listen to more live music. Applause is mother's milk to musicians. Unfortunately, most people don't know how to clap and produce a feeble smacking sound rather like a flounder flapping around on a wooden pier. There is a technique to clapping as there is to every aspect of life.

The old *Tonight Show* used to hire professional clappers. These used to be a staple of talent agencies and they would conduct clinics on how to clap for studio audiences. All the big studios employed professional clappers. These clinics date from the time of Shakespeare and the Globe Theater. Now they just flash a sign and hope for the best.

You clap by lightly cupping your hands and bringing one hand against the palm of the other *at a 45 degree angle so that the tips of one hand's fingers are striking the base of the other hand's fingers.* Staggered hands create a bubble-like chamber that produces a much sharper report than if the hands are brought together palm to palm and finger to finger.

CHAPTER 23
FROM OUT OF
THE ASHES

On January 23, 1978, Chicago's guitarist Terry Kath put a gun to his head, not realizing it was loaded, and pulled the trigger. Kath's loss had a profound effect on the group and may have been a factor in Chicago's tilt toward MOR power ballads as their bread and butter. The day after Kath's untimely death, a Chicago rep phoned Bill Champlin, head of the then-defunct Sons of Champlin, asking him to audition for the group. Champlin turned them down, In '81, Champlin hooked up with Chicago drummer Danny Seraphine with whom he wrote a few songs.

Seraphine began a campaign for Chicago to hire Champlin as lead singer and keyboard player. Robert Lamm objected. "What the hell do we need him for?" Cahmplin decided to give it a year. He ended up staying with the group through 2006. Champlin was instrumental in the writing of Chicago's many ballad hits, particularly those on *Chicago XXX* (2006), for which Champlin co-wrote four songs.

Can anybody recall those songs? No? How about "Saturday in the Park?"

The eighties were fallow ground for jazz rock. BS&T and Chicago continued to tour, finding new life in Europe. Champlin's Chicago contributions were not memorable, as he prepared for one of the greatest second acts in rock history, but the new Sons of Champlin was still years away.

The original Sons of Champlin (so named in honor of teenage husband and father Bill Champlin) made a splash with their debut double-album, *Loosen Up Naturally*. Although some critics called the Sons acid jazz, they were in fact all young hippy rock players. "If the Sons thought that Capitol wanted a spiritual flash, psychedelic messengers celebrating life, love and happiness, Capitol was probably more swayed by the fat sound of the three-man horn section." (Liner notes to *The Best of The Sons of Champlin* by Joel Selvin.)

These songs are deliriously good, dripping with sunshiny harmonies and good vibes. Although most of the songs are credited to a Steven Tollestrup, Champlin explains, "We were trying to inch around a former publishing deal. Anyway, I wrote all but 'Hello Sunlight' on the first album."

An ignorance of jazz tradition probably contributed to the freshness of the horn charts, which sound more like keyboard parts. As a result of this, and the stacked harmonies, the Sons had a unique sound. However, their limitations also held them back. Guitarist Terry Haggerty explained, "On 'Loosen Up Naturally' they played so great because they'd rehearsed it for a year. We taught them all the parts and they practiced. But when it came time to do new stuff, they couldn't do it." (Liner notes.)

There were no horn solos. Without improv ability, the band lacked one of jazz' primary building blocks. Nevertheless, *Loosen Up Naturally* is a delightful, *sui generis* record that stands up to repeated listening.

The eighties were a desert for jazz rock. Emilio Castillo discusses Tower of Power's dilemma at the time in the liner notes to *Dinosaur Tracks*. (Rhino.)

"To the industry at that time, it looked like we were the kiss of death. I am sure people looked at us and said, 'Well, there's got to be something wrong with them' and, indeed, there was a lot wrong with Tower of Power at that time. The band had various medical problems and personnel problems and legal problems. We certainly had our share of drug problems as well. Drugs had been a big role in pretty much the career of all the successful musicians of the late 1960s and throughout the 1970s, and it was true for Tower of Power as well.

"We had a lead singer that had, after he left the band and been gone from the band for four years, had become very seriously addicted to hard narcotics and wound up murdering three people. His name was Rick Stevens. He sang 'You're Still a Young Man,' and most of the songs on *Bump City* and also 'Sparkling in the Sand' from *East Bay Grease*. Great singer, a great guy, but just really fell prey to the drug thing.

"It became very difficult for us to get signed to another recording contract. Right about that time the disco thing had faded out. It was around 1980. We were looking for a record deal and down on our luck, to say the least. I had moved to Los Angeles to kind of get away from my own personal problems and try to get back in the business, as it were. I had a lot of friends down there....

"But getting back to that period we recorded some more tracks in 1983 at Dawn Breaker and we shopped them around again. We would get bites and nibbles from different companies. Polygram, I remember, was real close to signing us. They just wouldn't go out on a limb. Meanwhile all these new bands were comin' and goin', and Tower of Power still couldn't get signed.

"Pretty soon we did a few appearances on the *David Letterman Show* with the horn section. And there was a band, one of the new bands that had come out in the early eighties was a group called Huey Lewis and the News. They were from the Bay Area and it turns out they were huge Tower of Power fans. Huey asked us to record on his album. It was called *Picture This*....

"We did some more recording with them ... and they hit it really big with their album that had "I Want a New Drug" on it.

Huey came to us and he said he'd like to take us out on the road....

"It was already probably 1983 at that point, late '83, early '84. I made a deal with Huey Lewis. I said, "I will come out and I'll do the tour with you if you promise to promote Tower of Power as much as you possibly can." He literally went to the ends of the earth to resurrect Tower of Power. Every show he featured us. Several times during the set he introduced each person individually. He said the name Tower of Power repeatedly throughout the set. He talked about us in his interviews....

"And so things started to turn around for us and eventually, like I say, by the time 1988 rolled around, you know, people started referring to us as legends."

CHAPTER 24
CELTIC SOUL

The eighties were not kind to jazz rock but they were not without musical interest. Skinny tie power pop bands such as 20/20, The Knack, The Police, The Talking Heads and Elvis Costello gained currency.

Across the pond, Kevin Rowland dissolved one band and formed another. The new band was called Dexys Midnight Runners, after the popular drug Dexedrine. Formed in '78, they did not release their first album until *Searching For the Young Soul Rebels* in 1980. The band included trombone, sax and alto as well as keyboards and rhythm section. This isn't jazz rock but it's astonishing music and anybody who loves soul will love this.

From the liner notes: "Soon after a young bass player by the name of Pete Williams walked into the hideout carrying his tool under one arm and his complete Stax collection under the other. Disillusioned with new musak, he put his soul records on the table and shouted, 'I want to do something as good as these—only better.' The boys knew exactly what he meant and welcomed him with open arms."

Beginning with random snippets of radio as someone twists the dial, the murk and static abruptly pull into diamond-hard focus as Rowland announces, "For God's sake burn it down" and the horns sharply delineate soulful mesas. Rowland's rough voice is ideally suited to Celtic soul, a genre which, if he didn't create, he certainly defined. This obscure but rich style includes The Proclaimers (who might be Scots, but are soul brothers), Kokomo. and of course Van Morrison.

"Burn It Down" (formerly "Dance Stance") is unashamed of its Stax/Volt worship. "Shut your fuckin' mouth 'til you know the truth," Rowland growls. He's an Angry Young Man in the British tradition of Graham Parker, the novelist John Braine, the actors Lawrence Harvey and Richard Harris, and Elvis Costello, among others. Fortunately his anger morphs into something more positive with the second album, but let's not get ahead of ourselves for there is much to admire here.

The line-up also included Al Archer, organist Pete Saunders, drummer Andy Growcott, tenor player JB, alto player Steve "Babyface" Spooner, and trombone player Jimmy Paterson.

"Tell Me When My Light Turns Green" starts with an addictive horn line underlining Rowland's tortured vocal. Paterson adds a fleet solo leading into an *a capella* horn strut before the band falls back in. The horns are as much the point of the song as Rowland's singing. "The Teams That Meet in Caffs" is an instrumental that does for Celtic Soul what "Wipeout" did for surf music. Brooding horns and tremolo-rich organ define this irresistible slice of Celtic funk. Spooner solos substantially on alto.

"I'm Just Looking" begins with Rowland whispering in an Irish accent so thick you need a dictionary and a butter knife. "Geno" was the nearest thing to a hit on the record, an ode to Brit soul singer Geno Washington. With its classic bones and heartfelt everything, "Geno" is a memorable mid-tempo paean to clubbing. One can easily imagine Mick Jagger singing "Seven Days Too Long," a stomping soul smoker, although the major chords may have given him an upset stomach. Not Rowland, who's all over this like a cougar on a rabbit. Rowland has a unique voice—both rough and soulful. The closest thing to it is Felix Cavaliere, but unlike Felix, Rowland isn't afraid to let the roughness show. The *a capella* patch is killer.

"I Couldn't Help It if I Tried" is a mournful ballad suitable for a funeral procession in which Rowland sort of scats. "Thankfully Not Living in Yorkshire it Doesn't Apply" is a mellifluous falsetto flight of fancy with a joyful and infections hand-clapping chorus and a thrilling bridge. "Keep It" is a Stax homage on which Rowland lays down an inimitable vocal, lines curling up at the end with a duck's ass melisma. Horns choogle over a soulful fade-out. "Love Part One" begins with mournful saxophone and Rowland's spoken poison dart vocal to an ex-girlfriend, like something you'd hear in a beat bar in Greenwich Village in 1958. Finally, "There, There My Dear" takes off on horned wings for a rave-up belter with that characteristic Dexys horn chord.

Mission: create Celtic Soul. Mission accomplished.

DMR's next record saw an almost complete change in personnel, retaining only the trombonist Paterson, Rowland rebuilt the Runners with a string section and recorded their number one world-wide hit and the second most requested song at weddings, "Come On Eileen."

Even without "Come On Eileen" this is an astonishing record, beginning with the declarative "Celtic Soul Brothers." The band now included fiddlers Helen O'Hara and Steve Brennan from The Emerald Express as well as trombonist Paterson and reed players Paul Speare and Brian Maurice. "Brothers" begins with the violins sawing away over a folkie acoustic base leading into a killer melody with multiple chord changes.

"Let's Make This Precious" begins with a joyous upbeat horn fanfare that's about as far from Tower of Power's cerulean peacock tails as you can get. Paterson introduces the vocal with a rising 'bone wail. Precious is about putting your heart and soul into your work and it sounds it. It is a perfect marriage of style and subject. Rowland's voice bespeaks passion with every utterance. "First let's hear somebody sing me a record that cries pure and true/No not those guitars, they're too noisy and crude...." he sings unaccompanied over hand claps. The organ slides beneath and the whole band winds up for the biggest roundhouse hook in music when the strings abruptly sprout from the top. This is Rowland's greatest song and a perfect summation of his esthetic.

"All in All" begins with Rowland emoting over slow waltzing violin, a lyrical dirge with an arresting melody. "Jackie Wilson Said" is of course Van Morrison's song and many people don't think Rowland's version measures up because he doesn't do much with it, but the violins and the intensity of Rowland's vocal validate this version. The string section works hand in glove with the horns. "Old" shuffles at septuagenarian speed with respect and exquisitely blue horns straight from the Stax/Volt playbook.

The horns and strings briefly reprise "Precious," followed by a free-form rap set to strings, and then "Plan B" leaps from the speakers like a Pict warrior brandishing a sword. An unforgettable bridge with the lyrics "Bill Withers was good to me." When these collective mush mouths attempt to sing "Plan B," it sounds like "love fades." "Plan B" segues seamlessly into the soulful and hook-laden "I'll Show You" with its perfect Memphis horn chart.

"Liars A to E" has the slow power of a funeral train. Rowland's highly textured vocal sounds like a dramatic reading as he hurls his soul all over the room. "Until I Believe in My Soul" is the most nakedly emotional vocal in this bouquet of hothouse flowers, and that's saying something. The horns swagger with practiced authority as Rowland growls his disappointment at the world. Brian Maurice flies free on tenor for four bars then it's back to the grind. "That's all there ever is, Oh yeah, yeah yeah? That's all there ever was, yes, yes, ha ha ha." Plus the priceless muttered aside, "You've got to be fucking kidding me." It trails off into Rowland muttering to himself with a sweet string accompaniment lulling you into a false sense of calm before the band reasserts itself and Rowland resumes his self-mocking vocal.

Finally, there is "Come on Eileen," as infectious a song as any "one-hit wonder" ever had. Note the banjo adding its sweet voice to the mix and the Mark Twain-ish Big River banjo bridge. This may be the hookiest song ever recorded.

Dexys Midnight Runners were far more than one-hit wonders. *Too-Rye-Ay* remains the definitive Celtic soul statement.

CHAPTER 25
SIGNS OF LIFE

People bitch about the seventies. But it was the eighties that saw the rise of rap. Rap has its defenders, to be sure, but be honest. Can anyone imagine any rap "song" of whatever era being played and listened to with reverence a hundred years from now?

Oh honey, don't let me commence.

The Boxing Gandhis are a southern California band that issued their first album, *Boxing Gandhis*, in 1994 on Mesa. The band featured Alfred T. Ballesteros on vocals and sax, Steve Samuel on drums, Brie Darling on vocals and percussion, Ernie Perez on vocals and sax, David Darling on vocals and guitar, David Kitay on vocals and guitar, and Carl Sealove on bass. Their sound is a rich mix of jazz, soul and funk.

The Gandhis proudly compare themselves to George Clinton, Sly Stone, the Isley Brothers, James Brown, Marvin Gaye, War, Curtis Mayfield and Pops Staples. Good enough. But the Gandhis have a slinkier vibe than their soul heroes due to their hipster group vocals.

"If You Love me (Why am I Dying?)" is an environmental jeremiad but oh does it slink, with a clever vocal arrangement with Sealove's bass burbling up from the basement. They have the same poppy syncopated beat as Tower of Power, although the voicings couldn't be more different. "Lose My Language" continues the theme with this slow burner about alienation from nature. The horn arrangements are simplicity itself, with saxes holding a note through two measures. The hook comes in the form of a change-up launching a tenor on an extended one note excursion.

There is an anguished, searching quality to much of Boxing Ghandis' music. "In This House" is an exception, a cautiously optimistic ode to family unity in a bad neighborhood. "It's no pretty picture—I look out my door—It's so hard to keep it all at bay." This song begs for an uplifting sitcom starring Tracey Morgan and produced by Oprah to serve as the theme.

"Speak As One" is a delicate hipster anthem with a slow-moving hook that catches you on the point of the chin by surprise. Their offhand way of singing sort of slides into the tonic and sounds a lot like cats, or like a lot of cats. They share with Dan Hicks the knack of making their difficult music sound effortless, although they sound less forced. (I always had the feeling that the moment Hicks finished a take he ripped off his headphones and yelled, "WELL THAT WAS A GOATFUCK!")

"Again and Again" has that same easy, syncopated subtly powerful blues vibe. The band projects effortless power. They don't knock you over with trumpet fanfares, they suck you in with a natural rhythm and intimate vocals. David Darling, who wrote most of the material, has a sinewy voice that almost disappears in its own mannerisms. The song "Free" is their Summer of Love moment, sung by Brie, who has a similarly slinky sensibility.

"Interesting Again" is a terrific song about boozing, sung/rapped by Ernie Perez over an insinuatingly grimy sax. It sounds like a bar song but I can't imagine any bar allowing it—but maybe by the time they play it everybody's so shit-faced they don't even notice. There are no conventional romantic songs on Boxing Gandhis. "For Your Attention" is the closest they get.

In '96 Gandhis released *Howard* with an expanded band that included three saxes and a trumpet. "Piece In the Valley" is a mournful ballad about a guy with low self-esteem who loses his job, but that's okay, he's got a gun. "Promised Land" is a surprisingly jaunty indictment of politics and deteriorating civilization with an exquisite Dave/Brie harmony. "Sun Don't Shine On Everyone" is a funky rueful look at the homeless. Gandhis heart everyone. "Cuzacan" is the Gandhis' "Signs." "Why you always tryin' to sound like Sly?" they slyly ask themselves. The refrain is, "'Cause I can, 'cause I can" ("Cuzacan.") Alfredo Ballesteros blows a minimalist but very blue tenor solo.

Ernie Perez sings "Image of You" in falsetto, offering a palate-cleansing change from Dave Darling's more down and dirty vocals, horns bluesily swaying behind him. "Funky Little Princess" is about a teen runaway plaintively sung by Brie. These guys win the social consciousness sweepstakes hands down. Their sound is ideally suited for singing about the dispossessed with the creeping growl in their voices and those oh-so-lonely horns. "Far From Over" is about the undocumented workers' plight in America. "Fifty years of field work they say we don't belong here yet." No country on earth can endure if it loses control of its borders. So while we naturally sympathize with the plight of the downtrodden, could we have a little perspective please? Sometimes the Gandhis sound like one long bleeding heart lecture with a backbeat.

The Gandhis hint at a more playful side in their blips between songs such as "Just Another Week Part #3." Gandhis—take the rest of the week off! "Tell Me Why"—the world is unfair. Props for the great bridge.

"Love Her Too" is a welcome respite, opening with a rich mix of guitar and harmonica. Although there's a lot of similarity among the songs on this record, there's no denying that the Gandhis have created a unique and appealing sound from their individual voices. They don't get you out of your chair stomping, but they do get you leaning back and snapping your fingers.

Tower of Power released only two albums during the eighties: *Power* and the Sheffield Lab *Direct*. The brainstorm of Larry Brown, Sheffield was an early pioneer in direct to disc recording, and *Tower of Power Direct* is one of the earliest CD recordings by a pop band. It begins with the elegantly rousing fanfare segueing seamlessly into the joyful Castillo/Kupka writ "You Know It." Mike Jeffries is the lead singer here and like all TOP singers he's got the chops and a slightly mellower delivery than their current vocal powerhouse Larry Braggs. Albert King's "You're Gonna Need Me" is a rare straight-ahead blues that is good enough, but on a record of this brevity takes up space that could have gone to another original. At this point must submit Castillo/Kupka among the front rank of American songwriters, R&B zone.

Their signature instrumental "Squib Cakes" pops and soars and includes a Donald Byrd-inspired flugelhorn solo by Greg Adams before slowing *wayyy* down for Lenny Pickett's three a.m. tenor solo that swerves abruptly into six a.m. and three cups of coffee with Chester Thompson percolating on Hammond B3. Like so much of TOP's work, these songs are a more than adequate substitute for either coffee or 5 Hour Energy Drink.

A searing version of "What Is Hip" follows, Greg Adams' trumpet a blazing meteor leading the way. However, compared to recent recordings, *Direct* sounds muted, less effective than vinyl. The performances are magnificent as always but it sounds like you're standing outside the ballroom.

Malo recorded two albums during the eighties, *Malo V* and *Coast to Coast*, both of which are unavailable.

CHAPTER 26
SONS REBORN

By 1990 Bill Champlin had left Chicago to pursue a solo career. In 1997, just prior to reforming the Sons of Champlin, Bill recorded a live album called *Mayday*, which contains all the hallmarks of his new sound. The band consisted of Champlin on vocals and organ, Greg Mathieson on keyboards, Jerry Lopez on guitar and vocals, Rochon Westmoreland on bass, Eddie Garcia on drums, Tamara Champlin on vocals, and Tom Saviano on sax.

Saviano hovers over this session like a hawk, soaring, cajoling, leading and proving that in the right setting one horn is all you need. You hear the crackle of a small but enthusiastic audience. While the songs occupy the same cobalt hills and coulees as Tower of Power, each favors a different approach to songwriting. The Sons take a more intimate approach. They will draw you in with murmur while Tower of Power does its best to paste you to the wall.

Mayday begins with "Party Time in D.C.," a song that could not be more timely. Champlin, Lopez, and Tamara begin with *a capella* harmony before the band kicks in with an inexorable groove. "I've been sitting watching television watching some politician promise everything but the moon...." Lying politicians and the same old same old. Although Champlin's politics are progressive this song applies to all.

The next two songs feature a one-two punch constituting one of the greatest segues in musical history. "Lovers Tonight" and "Take It Uptown" share the same deep R&B sweetness and punch the Temptations used to turn out so effortlessly. "Lovers Tonight" begins with a joyful descending keyboard and guitar riff that blossoms with the addition of Saviano's tenor and Jerry Lopez' tensile vocal. Lopez sounds so much like Champlin it's eerie.

"Lovers" has a massive hook in the bridge followed by a soaring Saviano. The band switches up a key to the segue with a hortatory and ecstatic Saviano bursting into "Take It Uptown" (Champlin/Kenny Loggins), which sounds like the second movement of the funkiest suite you never heard. Saviano seizes the head and nails it to the sky. Champlin seamlessly picks up the vocal with his unique gritty undertones.

Does Saviano consider his work with Champlin jazz?

"Certain compositions with the Sons definitely felt like jazz. Now, the core of the songs had a jazz element to start with especially during improvisational sections. For me personally, I took what I was hearing and took it to where I thought it should go. The band usually went along with me (at least on the solos!)"

"Southern Serenade" is a sweet honey-dripper with Alan Toussaint's DNA. Great boy/girl vocals and gospel inflected bridge. Champlin bends his notes like he's making balloon animals for the kids. He'd probably not consider doing a solo performance but he sounds like he could pull it off.

Quincy Jones' "In the Heat of the Night" is just a man and his Hammond, churchy and funky, building momentum until the band slides under him like a surfacing killer whale. Lopez scats to his own guitar arcing streaks of blue light, stops singing and skims his guitar into one foaming blue wave after another.

Saviano, who has played with Ray Charles, Les McCann, Lee Ritenour, and Clarence Clemons, adds a surging, Henderson-influenced tenor solo to Champlin's "Headed for the Top."

"Another Day/Song for my Grandfather" features Greg Mathieson's bluesy jazz piano and Saviano intertwining their sounds for a mini suite. David Foster, Jay Graydon and Champlin initially wrote "After the Love Has Gone" for Champlin's solo record, but Maurice White heard the song and wanted to record it. Champlin said, "I'm not an idiot, man." So they gave the song to EWF. Champlin's version is grittier and less splashy but at least as effective.

"First and Last" could have come out of Tower of Power's playlist. You can practically hear the TOP horns. In other words it's funkified to the max and syncopated to give a chiropractor nightmares. Eddie Garcia and Rochon Westmoreland could be holding a rhythm clinic at Berklee in "Bass Solo," which is also drum solo. Rochon scats to his bass like Ella Fitzgerald using an octave foot pedal to double up his line.

Mayday is a snapshot of a band on the verge of renaissance.

Later that year Champlin reformed the Sons with Mic Gillette (Tower of Power, Cold Blood) on trumpet, Saviano on sax, Geoff Palmer on keyboards, Dave Schallock on bass, James Preston on drums, and Tal Morris on guitar. With some personnel changes they have been active ever since. It was this band that recorded *Secret* in 2002 Live at Meyer Sound Performance Hall.

"Hold On/For Joy" is a runaway train song with flags waving and horns blasting. Champlin's voice cuts like a musical saw as the train pulls into the station, turns around and leaves as "For Joy," a series of ascending blue-hued plateaus. Gillette and Saviano in tandem are smooth as ripping silk before yielding to a shredding Tal Morris solo.

Geoff Palmer wields Milt Jackson's vibes on the party anthem "Rooftop."

Like their Bay brethren TOP, The Sons' live albums are as tight as most bands' studio albums. This willingness and ability to throw down is one of the differences between a jazz rock band and a regular rock band. Michael Jackson spent hundreds of thousands of dollars recording his albums. So have many of the dinosaur industry's greatest carnivores. Jazz musicians, however, don't need a fancy studio, catered shrimp or an army of hangers-on. They come to play.

Tower of Power were extremely active during the nineties, touring constantly and recording five albums. They are all good records. Of these, *Tower of Power Live* is the most significant because it provides a snapshot of a working band in their normal environment and showcases the band's unbelievable tightness. Fittingly the cover art shows all those gleaming horns lined up and waiting.

Trumpeter Jesse McGuire introduces "Soul With a Capital S" with the showmanship of Michael Buffer that this punchy band certainly deserves. Lead singer Brent Carter is in an Apollo mood as he rocks it to the thick, sweet hook in the bridge and the band segues into "Oakland Stroke" on the outro. "I Like Your Style" is a celebratory song with lilting horns and gorgeous chords. "Soul Vaccination" dives deep into funk, opening with just drums and grunting baritone. One by one the other horns join in building to the catharsis in the bridge.

"Down to the Nightclub" features such extreme syncopation you should have a EMR team standing by while listening. The audience needs little urging to join in on claps. Brent Carter gives the ballad "Willin' to Learn" the old school treatment with just the right amount of melisma, while the horns unfold like rainbow. McGuire contributes an elegant trumpet solo. "Diggin' on James Brown" expertly replicates JB's horn style with the welcome addition of Doc Kupka rumbling below on baritone. It's a homage and a funky saga in its own right.

Listening to Tower of Power makes you hipper, younger, and better looking.

CHAPTER 27
ZAPPA AND STEELY DAN

As the book progressed friends kept suggesting bands. Two of the most frequently suggested are Frank Zappa and the Mothers of Invention, and Steely Dan. Being a huge Zappa fan, and having seen him in concert, I do not consider his tightly-controlled arrangements the stuff of jazz, although there is no question that many of his players had the chops and went on to play jazz.

Frank's guitar playing always struck me as technically proficient but emotionally void, with an endless string of harmonious licks but without peaks, themes, or climaxes. I'm not the person to make a case for Zappa as jazz.

Longtime news reporter and music writer Marc Eisen makes the case:

"He's definitely in there. *Hot Rats* has some serious jams. I think the two subsequent albums *Grand Wazoo* and *Waka/Jawaka* have their jazz moments. Remember that George Duke played in Zappa's band and he produced Jean Luc Ponty. I've never heard *Jazz From Hell*, but that came later. For me at least, Zappa is far more important than Chicago, which had one decent album and 25 bad ones. If "Willie the Pimp" (featuring Don Sugarcane

A Brief History of Jazz Rock

Harris) and the "Gumbo Variations" (featuring Ian Underwood blowing his brains out) aren't jazz improv, I don't know what is."

Mark the airline pilot says:

"If you remember, the Duke, Louie Armstrong, Lionel Hampton, and many others UP TO BEBOP used to play very rigid improv. Most of the old band members read music, and the Duke and Hampton used to fine musicians if they strayed from their queue. Up until bebop jazz was very rigid, but the standards we grew to love were not pieces of improv. Miles with cool, Bird with bebop, and Herbie provided outlines for their music, the Duke provided written score. Motown Records found a wealth of well educated jazz musicians who could sight read like no-one's business.

"How does this relate to Frank? Frank recruited people who impressed him. Not all of them read music, most did. Like Miles, Frank provided an Outline sketch (written of course, I have seen and even held a few when they were not worth much). Much like Miles he communicated what he wanted, and to survive as a musician had to produce. It was much the same with other bands. Zappa was also a drummer (not many people know that) and employed drummers who could play polyrythms. He also employed Ruth Underwood on vibraphones. "I never thought Gershwin sounded like jazz, and there are many in the classical camp that claim him. I guess some of it is impression!"

For the definitive word on Steely Dan I turned to one of the founding member of Firetown and Emperors of Wyoming, Phil Davis.

"In many ways, Steely Dan ARE jazz rock, though they were never a self-limiting or self-defined jazz rock band *à la* Dreams. But it's always there and has been from the start. In fact, they were extremely demanding on the talent they hired and looked toward the mastery of jazz players to live up to their perfectionist standards, since the slovenly world that is often rock recording never did meet them, nor did they ever feel comfortable there. In jazz, they found musicians with a higher calling, with chops and skills that surpassed their own as a matter of course. "For one, the obvious influences are there all along, as early as the very much jazz influenced guitar solo on their first hit single, "Do It Again," on to the *Pretzel Logic* with Jeff Skunk Baxter's wah-wah guitar version of "East St. Louis Toodle Loo," a Duke Ellington classic and of course *Aja*, the classic, with Wayne Shorter soloing, among other luminaries. Wayne Shorter, of course, is jazz royalty in most critic's books, so. I've included the Wikipedia run down of Aja and it's impressive. I would also point out that Fagen's debut solo record *The Nightfly* is permeated with jazz vibe, more so than rock, with a jazzy-blues version of "Ruby Baby" that could be covered by any self-respecting hard jazz combo. Originally done by the Drifters, and later Dion, written by Lieber and Stoller, "Ruby Baby" is a perfect example of the crosswalk influences of early '60s R&B, East Coast pop, and jazz. Of course Fagen's got both Brecker brothers and other jazz rock royalty on the record as well.

"Steely Dan employed some pretty stellar horn-session guys who definitely had Top Shelf jazz rock chops. You'd have to look at the names. But as an example, Fagan and Becker had to share song writing credits with Keith Jarrett, ultimately for plagiarizing the melody of "Gaucho." And let's not forget Sonny Rollins' stunning and unforgettable saxophone solo on the Rolling Stone's "Waiting On A Friend," from *Tattoo You*, or Ronnie Ross' "Walk on the Wild Side" sax coda for Lou Reed's classic, an improvisation that may indeed have gotten more airplay and widespread worldwide distribution than any single jazz horn solo in history."

CHAPTER 28
JAZZ ROCK IN THE 21ST CENTURY

There has been a paucity of jazz rock since the turn of the century but not a void. Sons of Champlin are back (completely reoriented from their original style) and both Tower of Power and Malo never went away. There must be something in that West Coast air that causes these bands to thrive.

By now TOP has accumulated a massive original catalog and has showed no signs of slowing down. *Oakland Zone* (2003) is one of their best. Larry Braggs appears for the first time on record as lead singer and charter members drummer David Garibaldi and guitarist Jeff Tamelier have rejoined the band.

The jacket displays the art deco marquee of the Fox Oakland Theater along with Jerry Brown's endorsement. "On behalf of the people of Oakland, I am proud to say that we are honored once again, to be the source for the unrivaled sound and rhythm of Tower of Power in the *Oakland Zone*."

Right on, Mr. Mayor! Now that you're governor, perhaps you could give a shout out to my homies the Plimsouls and call for a state-wide jazz rock competition. "Eastside," "Oakland Zone," and "...Eastside" are mostly instrumental exercises in booty-shakin' funk. "Oakland Zone," with its basso declarations is particularly droll.

"Life Is What You Make It" has a Family Stone vibe in its simple upbeat theme and wisdom before sliding into the that slippery Oakland Zone. "Happy 'Bout That" is one of those sunny day glad-to-be-alive songs that sounds like a mash-up between The Tempts' "My Girl" and the Impressions' "The Woman's Got Soul." If it weren't for the horns preeminent position this could have been a Motown release. The horns assert themselves in a stunning chorus.

"Stranger In My Own House" begins with ominously minor horns chugging beneath Bragg's lament. Doc Kupka's baritone rudely introduces the swaggering bridge. Doc's baritone sounds like a rutting boar in "Back in the Day," a tricky, fun-filled look back at the vast TOP catalog name-checking many of the songs.

Few bands can match TOP's enormous song book. In 2009, they recorded *The Great American Soul Book*, their first album of covers. Guest vocalists include Joss Stone, Tom Jones, Huey Lewis, and Sam Moore and guest musicians include George Duke and Bruce Conte.

Larry Braggs makes clear on "You Met Your Match" that he needs no help in the vocal department, nevertheless TOP have now entered that stage where they are legends and must stake their claim to the soul crown. Aretha Franklin recently released *The Great American Songbook* with "Try a Little Tenderness" and "It Ain't Necessarily So." Huey Lewis & the News released *Four Chords & Several Years Ago* with "Little Bitty Pretty One" and "Mother in Law." Same deal.

Tom Jones joins Braggs for the Sam & Dave standard, "I Thank You." It's outside TOP's comfort zone and they make it sound like a stroll in the park. The song's contours are much simpler than TOP originals. Braggs fares better on his own on "Loveland," a sweepingly romantic ballad. Joss Stone ("It Takes Two"), Sam Moore ("Mr. Pitiful"), and Huey Lewis ("634-5789") all make their marks, but the standout here is "Star Time (Tribute to James Brown)," a mash-up of "It's a New Day," "Mother Popcorn," "There it Is," and "I Got the Feelin'." TOP has Brown's pop and sizzle down better than Brown whose esthetic is closer to that of TOP than any other soul artist.

I don't mean to be heretical, but Larry Braggs is at least as good a singer as Brown was, and why isn't there a James Brown Experience like there are Beatles homage bands? (The Fab Four come to mind.) Something to do with rights no doubt. In the meantime, TOP's tribute could give the lambada lumbago.

In 2005, Malo recorded a live album at The Palace Indian Gaming Center in Lemoore, CA. *En Vivo/Live* is a vivid album of a working band at the top of its game. Jazz-wise, it's a match for *If Live in Europe*. If has the odd time signatures but Malo has that multi-rhythmic drum thing that is pure Afro-Cuban. Two conga players and a drummer talking to each another and playing tonally.

Beginning with "Momotombo," the record explodes and never lets up. Despite a propensity for stratospheric trumpet work the band never sounds shrill and their horn work is as tight as their Bay brethren, TOP. The horns never overpower the rhythm section.

Malo had flirted with rap previously to no good end. But "Ritmo Reggaeton" forgives all sins, opening with Octavio Garcia's sighing, cackling benediction. Guitarist Jay Rosette picks out a memorable riff introducing the rap. Rap in Spanish is highly palatable. Pianist Daniel Cervantes plucks a memorable counterpoint to Rossette's guitar.

Beginning with "Nena," the band tears through Malo classics "Cafe," "Sauvecito," Pana," and "Oye Mama" with grace and aplomb. Arcelio Garcia and Octaviano Garcia (no relation) space their vocals an octave apart and neither is afraid of tremolo. Arcelio is the low one. Just when you think the band is done they kick it into overdrive. Most of the songs are at least four minutes long permitting each instrumentalist brief but memorable statements, like Frank Bailey's stratospheric trumpet on "Cafe," and 'bonist Pete Rodriquez quoting "Dixie." "Cafe" is among their most Afro

Cuban compositions with a sizzling intro that stops short for one long pause. You can hear people holding their breath.

On Mother's Day, 1990, Chicago phoned Danny Seraphine and told him he was out of the group. He was dumbfounded. They'd sworn an oath to one another similar to that of the Three Musketeers. The band claimed that Seraphine's drumming had suffered of late and that is possible. Seraphine lived in Colorado for awhile then moved to Los Angeles where he became involved in producing and recording.

Seraphine began playing with a group of studio musicians and in 2006 he formed California Transit Authority with Larry Braggs on loan from TOP, guitarist Marc Bonilla, keyboard player Ed Roth, bassist Mick Mahan, and keyboard player Peter Fish. Response was sufficiently positive to warrant a record, *Full Circle*.

Here's all the redemption Seraphine needs. *Full Circle* is half re-imagining Chicago classics, half fresh material and totally original. It's a blast to hear a band other than Chicago performing these songs, and the spin Seraphine has put on each one. The record opens with Chuck Mangione's "Something Different," which instantly establishes Bonilla as a freak hybrid of Stevie Ray Vaughan, Stevie Vai, and Nuno Bettencourt. The guitar in concert with keyboard player Fish create a horn-section like wail.

But it's Terry Kath's "Introduction" with tenor player Brandon Fields, trumpeter Lee Thornburg and trombonist Nick Lane that will blow you away. They take it at a slightly faster tempo than the original. Seraphine sounds energized but not out front like Buddy Rich. There's an almost baroque structure to the song that the band expertly navigates, Seraphine turning it around with a gallop as the horns enter their fascinating labyrinth. The horns rear back for the next movement and Seraphine introduces a massive percussion hook with his tom-tom beat. Bonilla honors Kath's solo but adds his own twists as the sound builds and builds until the horns slide in and the song peaks in a stomping catharsis culminating in a drum solo.

Braggs gives "South Carolina Purples," a blues off the first album, a more soulful reading than even Kath could. Bonilla's exuberant version of "Make Me Smile" jumps out at you. Emotive guitar replaces the lead singer for this instrumental version and who needs a vocal anyway? Everyone who hears this will immediately conjure the lyrics.

Dave Boggia's "Several Thousand" gives us the band without any Chicago influence, a rich sound but basically a rock ballad with grafted horns. Braggs turns Greg Allman's "Dreams" into more of a singer's song simply through the strength of his performance. I would have preferred more Chicago or something fresh cooked up with the horns.

"West Virginia Fantasies" is part of James Pankow's "Suite for a Girl From Bohannon" (which is listed on the latest *Chicago II* reissue). Bonilla states the theme tartly over the bass line that every fan has committed to memory, but in doing it without the horns they've rethought the song, assigning horn parts to guitars and keyboards. The song slides into "Colour My World" as you expect, but not in an expected way. What sounds like a musical saw states the theme—sounds like a synthesizer until Bonilla dampens the electronic distortion and gets serious playing most of the song without accompaniment. It's a brilliant reinvention. Braggs croons the lyric when you least expect it sending chills down your spine. Bonilla fills the rest of the space with a lean, melodic solo.

"Happy Cause I'm Going Home" sounds like Spyro Gyra. Bonilla's "Antonio's Love Jungle" sounds like something the Jazz Crusaders might have kicked up. Seraphine dedicates his solo to "Papa Jo Jones, Papa Joe Porcaro, and Bernard Purdie." Conjure words to a drummer. Seraphine's drumming has the pop and sizzle of another Jones, Philly Joe.

Chicago did Spencer Davis' Group's "I'm a Man" on their first album. CAT play it live at the 2006 Modern Drummer Festival with the horn section and Keith Emerson replicating Winwood on his Hammond B-3. With Sheila E on timbales and Alex Acuna on congas, Seraphine engages in a tri-part conversation that recalls Art Blakey's experiments in rhythm.

A Brief History of Jazz Rock

Finally there is "25 or 6 to 4," also from the Festival. It rolls over you like a familiar surf shoving you down and dragging you back with it. Bonilla succeeds both in summoning Kath's spirit and being true to his own. No Chicago singer can hold a note as long as Larry Braggs.

In 2013, CTA released its second album, *Sacred Ground*. Guitarist Bonilla did the horn charts and they sound A LOT like early Chicago. Will Champlin, son of Bill Champlin, sings on "Sacred Ground" and many other tracks sounding nothing like his father while delivering spot-on emotional vocals.

The third song is Al Kooper's "I Love You More Than You'll Ever Know." I wish they would record the entire first BS&T album. Larry Braggs is a better singer technically than Kooper, and where Kooper landed on the beat Larry lags behind, which makes this an interesting and worthwhile interpretation. Will Champlin's "Strike" encapsulates this band with its passionate vocal and horns. The instrumental "Prime Time" shows off the horns. Bill Champlin sings the vocals on "Full Circle" with his characteristic tensile steel yet somehow warm voice. There are a couple other guest singers on the record and for the most part they knock it out of the park.

CHAPTER 29
THE TOP TEN GREATEST JAZZ/ROCK ALBUMS

"Of the making of lists there shall be no end." Sure it's entirely subjective and everyone will have their favorites. This is just my personal ranking, which is subject to change at any time.

ONE: *Chicago*. (Sometimes known as *Chicago II*.) The *Rhapsody In Blue* of jazz/rock uses jazz tropes that place the three horns front and center in this hortatory paean to activist America. There's a Mingus-quality in the complex swirl of individual voices. Just keeps getting better and better on repeated listening and contains the classics "Wake Up Sunshine," "Make Me Smile," and "25 or 6 to Four."

TWO: *Dreams*. Dreams triumphs on the basis of Kent's and Lubahn's jazzy, hook-laden comps, the deliriously free-blowing of the Brecker Brothers on horns and Billy Cobham's Philly Joe-inspired beat.

THREE: If: *Europe '72*. Hard to believe this is only seven guys, and that includes a singer who doesn't play. European audiences are more tolerant of free blowing, which means these live recordings run long, with "What Did I Say About the Box,

Jack?" running over twenty minutes. The supple two-man horn section is reeds only.

FOUR: Malo: *En Vivo*. This Afro/Cuban blowout recorded live at The Palace Indian Gaming Center explodes like an incendiary piñata. Among the tightest improv an ensemble playing you will ever hear. Trumpet and two trombones meld J.J. Johnson and mariachi music and the rhythm section is as complex as anything by the Afro-Cuban All Stars or Tito Puente.

FIVE: Tower of Power: *Live*. Continuing our predilection for live recordings because let's face it—jazz players have an advantage here. It contains many of their classics including "What Is Hip," "So Very Hard to Go," and "Down to the Nightclub." Tight and syncopated.

SIX: Butterfield Blues Band: *In My Own Dream*. I don't even own this record. The cheapest copy I can find is thirty bucks, but most of it is available on the more widely available *Anthology*. Butterfield stretches his writing chops on the brilliant title tune with its iconic Dave Sanborn sax solo and the wrenching blues-plumbing "Last Hope's Gone."

SEVEN: Blood, Sweat and Tears: *Blood, Sweat and Tears*. Their second album found the band reborn and reformed with new personnel, notably David Clayton-Thomas on vocals, and a more freewheeling approach to improv, particularly among the horns. Songs like "God Bless the Child" and "Spinning Wheel" will be with us always.

EIGHT: The Electric Flag: *Long Time Comin'*. Bloomfield brings the raga, particularly on the eight-minute "Another Country," but the whole album is drenched in soul with tight, Watt/Stax-inspired horn charts and outstanding ensemble work.

NINE: Mogul Thrash: *Mogul Thrash*. When Fernando Perdomo first told me of this band, formed by former members of Colosseum, King Crimson and the Average White Band, I was dubious. *Mogul Thrash* is a brilliant jazz/rock synthesis with long tracks that allow the soloists plenty of room and ensemble playing that's as tight and galvanizing as James Brown.

TEN: Blood, Sweat and Tears: *New Blood*. There was another massive personnel shuffle for the fourth album, with Jerry Fisher in as lead singer and Georg Wadenius on lead guitar. There's a lot of good stuff here but the *coup de grace* is the one/two punch of Carole King's "Snow Queen" segueing into Herbie Hancock's "Maiden Voyage."

www.ingramcontent.com/pod-product-compliance
Lightning Source LLC
Chambersburg PA
CBHW020418080526
44584CB00014B/1393